GARDENING
IN THE
SHADE

GARDENING
IN THE
SHADE

By Harriet K. Morse

❖ REVISED EDITION ❖

TIMBER PRESS
Beaverton, Oregon
1982

COPYRIGHT © 1962 HARRIET K. MORSE

COPYRIGHT 1939 CHARLES SCRIBNER'S SONS

This edition is reprinted by
TIMBER PRESS
through arrangement with
CHARLES SCRIBNER'S SONS, 1982

Library of Congress Cataloging in Publication Data

Morse, Harriet Klamroth, 1891-
Gardening in the shade.

Reprint. Originally published: New York:
Scribner, 1962.
Includes index.
1. Gardening in the shade. 2. Shade-tolerant
plants. I. Title.
SB434.7.M67   1982   635.9'54   81-23231
ISBN 0-917304-16-0   AACR2

PICTURE CREDITS

Molly Adams: frontis, 107, 121
Lynwood M. Chace, from National Audubon Society: 43
Paul E. Genereux: xiv, 29, 56, 67-top and bottom, 81, 99, 102, 126, 150
John H. Gerard, from National Audubon Society: 31
Gottscho-Schleisner: 2, 20, 34, George F. Hinrichs, designer, 131
Grant M. Haist, from National Audubon Society: 53
Black Star Photo by Henry M. Mayer: 38, top
Frederick W. Raetz: 148
Leonard Lee Rue III, from National Audubon Society: 38, bottom
Roche: 6, 13, 24, 87, 91, 96, 114, 139, 146

✢ CONTENTS ✢

v

✤ LIST OF ILLUSTRATIONS ✤

vii

✤ INTRODUCTION ✤

The shaded garden has character. It is cool and inviting on a warm day in midsummer. The gardener at work is grateful for shelter from the burning sun, while the stroller rejoices that flowers will prosper in all the tones and undertones of shade. The checkered patterns of sunlight and shadow play upon flowering shrub and herbaceous border, on path and pool and woodland walk.

Nature well provides us with material for creating beauty in shaded areas, if only we will analyze her laws for correct combinations. Shade has its vagaries, for it comes and goes, and who can pin it down? We do know that there are plants to fit practically every condition of shade, and I hope in this work to prove that there are a great many ways to clothe the "wilderness and the solitary places."

It is hoped that the ideas contained in this book will be useful to those who have gardens in the shade. The reader will understand that in a work of this character, exhaustive directions for all phases of culture are hardly possible. Such information must be sought in general books on gardening. The reader is referred to the second part of this work if he wishes to acquaint himself with the main characteristics and temperamental demands of all plants mentioned throughout the text, and many others not in the text.

There is hospitality the world over, and gardeners open wide their gates to us. Garden pilgrimages become increasingly popular, and thus do we acquire new points of view.

To the gardener who explores in foreign parts there are no language barriers to plant names. That bugbear, scientific nomenclature, stands him in good stead. Travelling in the Americas, in Europe, in Asia, if he asks for Myosotis scorpioides semperflorens any one who knows his botany will realize that he is merely asking for a variety of that shade-loving little plant commonly known as forget-me-not.

In almost any garden in America, flowers and shrubs may be found whose ancestors came from the Far East. For those who are garden-minded, travel in the orient has its special pleasures, for here one sees familiar friends in their native environment—forsythia—azalea—chrysanthemum—peony. Our late Ernest Wilson is responsible for the introduction to America of no less than 1000 new varieties from the Far East.

Among the many choice gardens to be seen in Japan, a Moss Garden had for me its peculiar allure. Imagine a dewy wooded glade at the foot of a precipitous hillside. A rocky cascade and a pool are there, but no waterfall. Instead, the rocks are clothed in sheets of emerald moss and dripping lichens. They seem to ripple into the pool and lap its edge as they play a sylvan symphony in tones of green. This entrancing spot is a sanctuary where mosses of many kinds are gathered together. They carpet the entire ground and clothe each rock with verdure. I enjoyed this shaded dell, dappled in sunshine, and watched a gnomish trio of Japanese, on their knees, and in silence meticulously plucking weeds. The whole spirit of this charming scene, so cool and green and still, spelled—peace.

There is beauty in the walled courtyards and terraces in China. In place of lawns, stone paving is used, and a picturesque tree dominates the scene. Fine color effects are produced by compositions of flowering plants in pots, while at odd corners little perennials crop up between chinks in the wall and stonework. The brilliant sun, as it shines through rich verdure, makes possible the most alluring shadow pictures on wall and terrace.

That the British have a flair for gardening cannot be denied by those who know the countryside and have seen what it produces. Observe the tiny back yards near railroad tracks, see the flora at Wisley and Kew, the forests of southern England, and the great historic parks and private estates. Everywhere, if we look, we find something which grows in the shade.

My impressions of Ireland are vivid still. I remember the stately

Irish yews in the gardens near Killarney, and in the shadow, great colonies of royal-fern, then a superb massing of fuchsias in vivid bloom. The deciduous woods in their dewy splendour encourage the prodigious growth of small-leaved ivies. They not only carpet the forest floor, but clamber happily over all the tree trunks and into the branches. The predominant color note everywhere is green—Irish green.

A trip to Germany could not be complete, it seems to me, without a visit to the Black Forest. One summer on a pilgrimage to that country I motored for miles upon fine roads, over hilltop and into valley, through glorious beech and hemlock woodland, cool and well groomed, where shafts of sunlight enliven the shadow. Here the floor was carpeted in evergreen needles and there with moss-grown boulders and whorls of ferns. In travelling swiftly along I wondered what those streaks of rosy lavender could be which at intervals clothed the roadside. Heather, of course.

I set out alone one day for an intimate acquaintance with the tiny flowers of the forest. I found them growing sparsely in the lighter spots, so I gathered them up—one specimen of a kind. Absorbed in my plant hunting zeal, I soon lost my way. Being alone and lost in the Black Forest so stimulated my sense of adventure, that I felt a little sorry when I presently sighted smoke curling from the chimney of a small roadside inn. I was still clutching the wilted bouquet, by this time no "artistic arrangement." I then regaled myself with a pot of tea, counting my treasures the while. I lined them up on the table, these wildlings in captivity, and this is what I had:

Bluebell	Cinquefoil	Wild geranium
Aster	Wild bleeding-heart	Cuckoo-flower
Fumitory	St. Johnswort	

(None of these plants is injured by moderate picking of its flowers.)

In all the world where is there more variety in natural beauty than right here in our own country? Gardening enthusiasm grows apace, and some day perhaps we in America will become as garden conscious as the British. The general topics of conversation on the commuters' trains to London are politics—and gardening. They talk about their bulbs, and so do we, but bulbs of another kind perhaps. However, great things are being done here, and art goes into the garden. We hybridize, we naturalize, we introduce good companions from foreign lands. Do we nurture our native flora? Do we realize that where one trillium flower is plucked from the wild, the plant may not bloom for several years? It would be deplorable if trailing arbutus, false Solomons-seal, lady-slippers, bittersweet, groundpine, and so many other plants in need of conservation were eventually to disappear entirely from our woodlands. One sees so much of our native heritage gathered from the wild, and cannot help wondering when the public will learn the damage it unwittingly is doing.

In a series of suggestions for clothing the shaded landscape, I have transferred from my mind's eye to paper many planting schemes, with a hope that the reader, through imagery, might be fired to carry at least some of them to fruition. In *Walden* Thoreau says, "If you have built castles in the air, your work need not be lost; that is where they should be. Now put foundations under them."

✦ ACKNOWLEDGMENTS ✦

To the many authorities consulted in the preparation of this book, I have pleasure in expressing my gratitude. I am especially indebted to the following experts in the field of botany, horticulture and design who have generously given their time to the reading of the manuscript. Their suggestions and kindly criticism have been of very real value. They are E. J. Alexander, Associate Curator at the New York Botanical Garden, Mary Deputy Cattell, Landscape Architect, Benjamin Blackburn, Adjunct Professor of Botany at Drew University and Thomas H. Everett, Assistant Director (Horticulture) and Senior Curator of Education at the New York Botanical Garden. Other authorities upon whom I have called for advice are Fairman Furness, Frederic H. Leubuscher and the late Henry Tubbs. I should like also to thank Theodora Barnwell for valuable suggestions, and Elizabeth C. Hall, librarian of the New York Botanical Garden, for her many kindnesses.

PART ONE

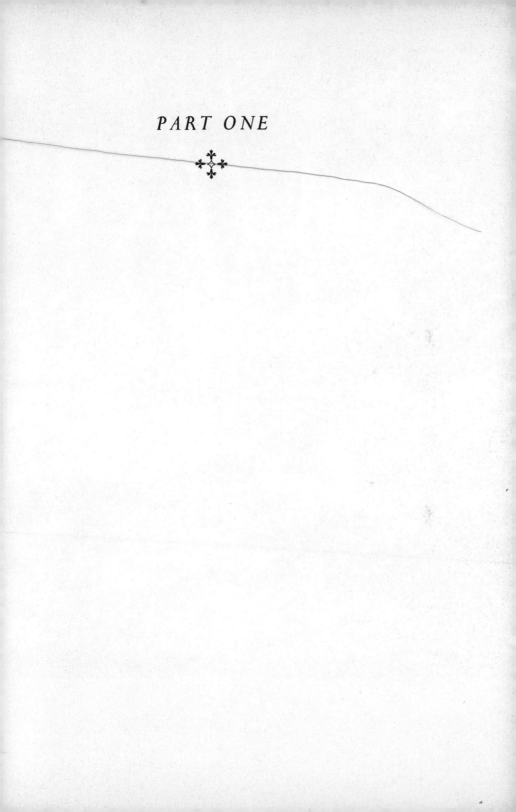

SHADE AND ITS VARIATIONS

I wish that shade might be cut and dried and labelled in a very definite sort of way. A photographer uses a light meter to determine the length of his exposures in a given light. It might be interesting were some one to experiment with such an instrument to determine with scientific certainty just how far one might venture with shade in the plant world. Some day an expert will write a treatise on the subject—or perhaps he has already done so.

In the meantime shade remains so illusive that in whatever category we place it there is often that "but" to be considered. To say that a plant will grow under trees does not make sense, for the shade under a narrow columnar tree might be no shade to speak of, whereas the shade of a beech might be black in summer and in spring there will be no shade there at all. Trees with tall trunks which branch high create a light shade when the sun is overhead, while trees with short trunks and spreading low branches may create a very full shade. Then there are those with sparse leafage like the pin oak, black locust, or sycamore, and others with denser foliage, like the ash.

In view of all this (and a great deal more), I have felt it simplest to divide shade into three main categories—full —light—half, with again certain unavoidable reservations. There is no point in being too dogmatic, for the gardener will use his own judgment, and study his locations carefully before setting out his plants. If he is very eager to meet with success in the shade, he will study his locations in summer, and find out where the shadows fall at various times of day.

Further meditations upon the vagaries of shade reveal other factors. There are plants which demand spring sun and are not particular what shade falls upon them the rest of the season—this includes most of the early spring bloomers. Other plants want spring sun, and light or half summer shade—those are mostly midseason flowering plants. Then there is winter shade or perpetual shade, as of buildings, walls, banks, and the shade cast by evergreens.

Of all the various degrees of shade there is one condition which few plants will tolerate, and that is all-year-round shade which is absolutely dense. This is found under spreading evergreens or on the north side of high walls closed in by low-branching overhanging trees. Such a condition may be extremely suffocating to plant life.

Then, also, many a plant dies in the shade, not because of the shade condition but from insufficient moisture and nourishment. Smaller plants should not be expected to live under extremely shallow rooted trees which take all the nourishment. Plants which may be tolerant of these most extreme conditions of shade are: moneywort (Lysimachia), Canada mayflower (Maianthemum) whose leaves disappear in summer, English ivy, periwinkle, pachysandra, American yew, and a few ferns such as Christmas and interrupted—but not under Norway maples. It is possible that some of these might even grow on a starvation diet, but I do not hold out much hope. They might be tried, for experiments are always interesting.

The shade spot in a sunny garden is the problem which faces most gardeners. They try their luck with sun lovers, hoping for miracles which just do not happen. The plants languish and die, or live such nostalgic lives, they were better dead. Finally the gardener, his patience exhausted, gives up, and leaves the shady spots—just bare.

One has, let us say, a garden on level ground with beds in more or less conventional arrangement. A large tree throws part of the planting space into shadow. A great deal of material exists which might live happily and prosper in that shadow. In wishing to retain the mood of the sunny bed as it transcends into shadow, one may have shade-tolerant varieties of a great many brilliant garden favorites which will grow in light or half shade, such as certain phlox, bluebells, foxgloves, and lilies.

There is no denying that Nature has her partialities. She does on the whole favor her growers-in-the-sun by giving them great vigor and brilliancy, but, even so, cultural rules must be obeyed. In this book, there are a great many plants mentioned which will grow in the sun as well as in the shade. I have endeavored to avoid listing those plants which merely endure the shade, though many of these here included would as willingly or rather be where there is sun. Some plants actually prefer growing in the shade, such as rhododendron maximum, English and American yew, maple-leaved viburnum, mountain-laurel, box huckleberry, leucothoë. The shade-preferring ground covers include trailing arbutus, wintergreen, periwinkle, pachysandra.

There are many herbaceous plants of the deep woodland association which actually prefer shade. Some of our most popular garden favorites such as plantain lilies (Hosta) and tuberous begonias ask only for good bright light. This is also the plea of most of our foliage house plants, and as everyone knows, the majority of ferns care little for sun.

Day-lilies provide a long season of bloom in a great variety of colors and forms.

SHADE TABLE

FULL SHADE

(*a*) Perpetual shade or winter shade caused by evergreens, high wall or building facing north.

(*b*) Shade under trees which cast a deep shadow in summer.

Note—For plants which stand the extreme condition of dense shade under surface rooting trees, see list on page 4.

LIGHT SHADE

(*a*) Among deciduous trees which branch high.

(*b*) Among deciduous trees with foliage which is not heavy.

(*c*) In such a situation where there is practically no direct sun but where the sun's rays filter through the leaves from time to time.

(*d*) On the north side of a low obstruction which causes a light airy shade, and where one feels the nearness of the sun, or the reflection of the sun. A cheerful shade in strong bright light.

(*e*) Where there is filtered sunshine or flashes of sun from time to time, probably never more than an hour or two a day—if one were to add it up.

(*f*) The shade of distant trees or buildings.

HALF SHADE

(*a*) Either morning or afternoon sun or intermittent sun coming and going.

(*b*) On the east or west side of a wall, hedge or house.

Note—Assuming that in June when the days are longest the sun shines about twelve hours, Half Shade would therefore mean not above six hours shade, and preferably less. Of course late afternoon sun is not very powerful.

2

SOILS AND THEIR TREATMENT

Bed and Board for Shade-Lovers

The well-being of plants depends upon the chemistry of the soil in which they live. It depends upon their exposure to light and air, to nourishment which they take in liquid form, to the texture of the soil and to proper drainage. Nature undisturbed attends to all this in her own miraculous way, through ecological associations, *i.e.*, in the relationship of vegetable organisms to their environment. She has made some plants so versatile that they are completely indifferent to their surroundings, but she would never think of permitting a showy lady-slipper to wave in the breeze on top of limestone rock in the blazing sun. The habitat of this flower is in the sheltered crannies of dewy woodland, rooted in rich moist soil. One cannot ignore these botanical laws if success is expected in the garden. It is not a complicated matter, this question of diet and health. One need be neither dietician nor gastronome to understand and enjoy this study in soil combinations.

Like human beings, plants breathe and drink. From the air they acquire carbon, oxygen, and nitrogen, from water they take hydrogen and oxygen, and the soil supplies them with chemical combinations, varying according to their type and temperament.

No matter what manner of garden you have, whether long established or one not yet in the making, it is well to set out with a shovel and start investigating the various types of soil in the undeveloped areas and in those spots where plants are growing unsuccessfully in the shade. This stock-taking may be enlightening, and a revelation to the inexperienced. Examine the earth to a depth of not less than nine inches in the unprofitable flower bed in the shade, in the places where grass grows poorly, in the damp spots at house angles, under evergreens, in those dreary places where you have not had courage to plant anything. Run your fingers through the little heaps of earth which have been piled up beside the hole, and study texture and color and you will learn a great deal. Examine the hole itself and acquaint yourself with the different layers of earth, and study the quality of the subsoil. This intimate contact with the earth and rolling it between the fingers as you test it will no doubt have its therapeutic value on your own well-being, as on the future well-being of all those plants which will make their home in the soil you are going to prepare for them.

TEXTURES AND NOURISHMENT

Sandy Soil. Sandy soil is, of course, very gritty and, dry or wet, falls apart in the fingers. The grains may run from coarse to very fine. Many plants will grow well in sandy soil, but where the rain runs off too quickly, it carries with it nourishment needed for plant development. It follows also

that the soil will dry out too fast. Sandy soil may be altered
by the admixture of peat moss or humus for their retentive
and organic properties. Top soil may also be added.

Clay Soil. Clay soil has no grit at all, even if one should bite
into it. It is stiff and plastic, and dry lumps, almost as hard
as cement, can scarcely be crushed between the fingers.
Very few plants will grow well in real clay; though it may
contain some nourishment it is too dense or heavy to allow
for proper drainage and root growth. It may be improved
by having mixed with it sand, peat moss and other humus
carriers, thus fitting it for shrub planting or for certain
herbaceous perennials.

Black Waxy Soils. Black waxy soils are the result of too much
humus and an overabundance of moisture. These need a
thorough plowing for aeration, and, if possible, to be
left so over the winter to allow the snows and frost to
improve and break them up. When ready for use, sand may
be added for lightness, and thoroughly decayed leaf mould,
or a bit of good friable garden soil, would improve the
texture.

Sour Soil. Sour soil is that which has gone beyond a healthy
degree of acidity and is dead. Sometimes even the necessary
bacteria cannot live in such soil. This condition may be
caused by insufficient light and air, improper drainage (from
which results an over-accumulation of water), and by
general neglect. Such soil had best be replaced by a good
healthy soil. If this involves too much expense, the sour soil

may be removed in part; the remainder, slightly limed, may have mixed with it a light friable loam which will be rich in bacteria and health-giving properties. A good plowing and exposure would be helpful. (In order to determine the condition of the soil see "Soil Testing and Rectifying," on page 19.)

Top Soil. Top soil, as the name implies, is the upper stratum of the earth's surface, which varies in make-up according to the locality in which it is found. Under heavy vegetation, as under forest trees, it is rich in organic matter. Top soil may be clayey or sandy or peaty. Under cultivation, that is, through manipulation and aeration, it improves and becomes the loam or good garden soil in which most of our plants flourish.

Good Garden Soil or Loam. Good garden soil or loam is loose and light and friable. It contains plenty of nourishment. It should be deep and well drained and it should retain sufficient moisture without being damp, and yet it will not dry out too rapidly. This is an ideal soil in which the majority of herbaceous perennials and shrubs will be happy. Yet this is not at all the soil to suit many of the broadleaf evergreens. Ericaceous plants prefer, some even demand, an acid tang to their diet, and porous texture, made up largely of decomposing roots and fibers.

Leaf Mould. Decayed leaves accumulate year after year on the woodland floor, and form, together with other decomposed matter, a soil usually high in nutritive quality, and this, when thoroughly decayed, is of a light and spongy character, retentive of moisture.

Humus. Humus is decayed vegetable matter or animal residues, which have been transformed into a rich dark organic material, by the breaking-down action of bacteria and other agencies. It is highly nutritive and has the capacity to retain moisture. Manures become humus when they are thoroughly decomposed.

Compost. The provident gardener lets nothing go to waste which might contribute to the health and well-being of his garden. A compost pile will bring valuable soil-building and mulch materials to his plants. He may build, hidden from view and in a shaded place, a receptacle for the accumulation of lawn clippings, weeds, kitchen refuse, spent flower stalks, etc., but no diseased materials.

A receptacle is not absolutely necessary but it is recommended because of its neat appearance and its protection of the composted material from washing away in heavy rains. Cinder block, brick or similar masonry may be laid without mortar in a square or oblong, one dimension being at least four feet wide, or prefabricated picket fencing may be used with a post at each corner.

There is no set rule for the building up of a compost heap. Some gardeners cover the pile with earth from time to time. They add wood ashes or manure when available, they sprinkle complete fertilizer, perhaps superphosphate, or lime, or pulverized animal manure. Many add from time to

time a commercially compounded material to hasten decomposition.

The compost should be kept moist at all times, if not by
rain then by the garden hose. The pile may be turned over
with a pitch fork at intervals. When several feet high it may
be covered with a thick coat of soil, smoothed flat or
slightly concave on top, and a new pile started. It is difficult
to determine just how long a time it will take for the
compost to become completely decomposed, perhaps four
to six months or maybe longer. However long it takes, it is
well worth waiting for.

Peat. Peat is decayed vegetable matter usually found in bogs
(but upland peat is found where the heaths grow and this
type of peat is strongly acid in reaction). Peat is sold
commercially, as everyone knows, under the name of Peat
Moss. This is used to render the soil friable and to make it
more retentive of moisture. When shrubs are newly planted,
many of them, especially moisture loving ones, benefit by
having peat moss worked in about their roots. As a top
dressing, peat is largely used for the majority of plants. It
should be mixed with soil, or a little soil is placed over it,
otherwise it tends to absorb for itself all the moisture after
a light rain, and the plant will have none. Its reaction is
slightly acid. One of its best uses is as a top dressing in
spring for laurel, rhododendron, and allied plants.

Mulch. A mulch is a covering or top dressing which helps
deter plant evaporation while allowing air to be admitted.
Materials usually employed as a mulch are rotted manure,

peat, straw, leaves, wood chips, hulls and others. Their complete decomposition will improve the structure of the soil.

Subsoil. Subsoil is usually not good for the growing of herbaceous perennials, but deep rooted shrubs and trees normally have their roots anchored in the subsoil.

Hardpan. Below the subsoil lies an earth stratum which may be extremely hard—almost like cement, sometimes. It is devoid of organic matter, and unless it is very far below the surface it may interfere with the proper drainage necessary to plants.

FERTILIZERS

Most plants while growing respond to fertilizers provided one does not apply them directly to the root.

Manures. Barnyard manures, often difficult to procure are, when available, of importance in maintaining soil fertility. They supply soil nutrients, humus and beneficial bacteria. They are primarily soil conditioners. Peat moss is a fair substitute, but to be effective as a nutrient the peat should have some sort of fertilizer added. Manures should be applied for the most part when moderately rotted. Fresh manure as a top dressing, especially to evergreens, may be absolutely fatal. One summer I saw a glorious composition of rhododendrons carefully planted on an estate near by. The next spring every shrub was dead. Upon inquiry I learned that these newly planted evergreens had been smothered with mounds of fresh manure, and so—were killed with kindness. I have seen the same thing happen, not with manure this time but with a heavy coating of lime—sure death to conifers and heaths.

Liquid Manure. Liquid manure is of excellent use. A barrel may be partly filled with manure, or a good sized burlap sack of manure may be laid or suspended in a barrel, the latter then filled with water, and allowed to stand a few days, and perhaps stirred occasionally. The mixture may then be diluted and applied to whatever plants are in need of stimulation. Where manure is unavailable, commercially dehydrated cattle manure could be used.

Commercial Fertilizers. The average gardener finds it practical to buy commercially prepared fertilizers made from animal manures in dehydrated, shredded or pulverized form. There are a great many other kinds of prepared products with or without definite reaction upon the soil. For instance dried blood or sulfate of ammonia are acid in reaction, while nitrate of soda, calcium nitrate or raw bone meal create an alkaline condition.

For instance, a commercially marketed compound such as 5-10-5 will contain 5% nitrogen, 10% phosphorus and 5% potassium plus other elements of great importance to plant development. Nitrogen stimulates the color of flowers and the size of leaves. Phosphorus strengthens root, flower and stem development. But too much phosphorus can cause yellowing of foliage and stunting of growth.

Potassium tends to strengthen, helps repel disease, promotes color of fruit and aids plants to withstand low temperatures. Generally, fertilizers are applied prior to the flowering season, at the rate of approximately two to three pounds per hundred square feet. The ground should be wet before application of the fertilizer, and gently but thoroughly watered afterward. Liquid fertilizers are usually applied at intervals of a few weeks during the growing season. Commercial fertilizers are most effective in the garden when the soil is already supplied with organic matter. In a sandy soil lacking in humus, the fertilizer would tend to dissolve and drain away.

In some sort of storage place, toolhouse, or garage, many gardeners find it convenient to have a row of galvanized ashcans with tops, or built-in bins. Here they have carefully labelled supplies of various fertilizers, lime, sand, compost, peat moss, and topsoil (uncovered). A mixture of topsoil, peat moss and sand, in approximately equal proportions, will be very useful, especially for tucking in about little perennials which have been heaved up by frosts or after heavy rains.

CHEMICAL CONTENT

Soils are neutral, sweet, acid, or sour, depending upon various factors, sometimes discernible, but usually not. If evergreens are indigenous to your locality, especially the cone-bearing kinds, such as pines and hemlocks, your soil is probably on the acid side. It may be intensely so, if there is a close dense shade. In such cases, you might find dampness and moss or fungus, but not necessarily. This condition may exist in virgin woodland, or even in dank neglected spots in cultivated gardens. Here the soil may have turned sour, a condition discussed on page 10. Where oak trees abound a reasonable amount of acidity may be expected, yet, near by, under an elm, or certain ash and locust trees, the soil may be alkaline (sweet or limy). In a bright airy garden where leaves are carefully combed away in autumn, the soil will very likely be neutral, perhaps even slightly alkaline, especially if lime has been regularly broadcast.

So many plants in the shade-tolerant class seem to demand acidity in varying degrees, and probably not more than half a dozen demand an alkaline condition. A great many plants will appreciate a mild acidity; some actually insist upon intense acidity. The majority of plants, however, are content with neutral soil, and happily, some are completely indifferent one way or the other.

Acidity in the soil will be found, as we have said, under such trees as the hemlock, mountain-ash, some of the oaks, many pines, spruces, white cedar, striped maple, sweet birch and others. Sometimes the tannic content from the bark and leaves is carried into the earth by rain-water, or the decomposition of leaves and bark creates the acidity. It seems that science has not yet proven just how much the plants themselves contribute to the soil acidity or how much depends upon the rocks from which the soil was derived.

If you know the soil requirements of your plants you will fit them to the soil which they crave by planting them in such places where the proper conditions exist, or, not content with that, you may create soil conditions to their liking.

Soil Testing and Rectifying. There are several ways of testing soil to determine its chemical status. The old litmus paper scheme is still used to some extent, though it is not usually recommended by the agricultural stations. A number of soil testing sets are on the market from which one may obtain fairly accurate results. The safest procedure might be to communicate with the nearest county agent, who will have your soil tested. Some of the fertilizer companies which have laboratories may assist you. Specimens of soil will be taken and tested, and according to the report you will know if your soil is acid, alkaline or neutral. If you yourself gather the soil to be tested, samples should be taken from different sections of the soil in question, and to the depth of 6 to 8 inches. All this will be mixed together thoroughly and then a one pound sample made from the combined soils.

The chemical condition of the soil is indicated by the letters pH. Neutral soil registers pH 7. From 7 to 9 indicates degrees of alkalinity. As the numbers decline below 7 and down to 4 they register the degrees of acidity present.

To create an alkaline condition, ground limestone is usually incorporated into the soil or used as a top dressing. Ordinarily a good thorough liming need be done only every few years, depending on the soil test.

Neutral or alkaline soil may be rendered acid by proper application of either sulfur, aluminum sulfate, iron sulfate or ammonium sulfate. The amounts vary according to the type of soil and its condition.

An acid reaction may also be produced by mixing with the soil, pine or hemlock needles, partially decayed wood from old stumps, especially from evergreens and oaks, and

Rhododendrons, mountain-laurel and azaleas with an under-planting of
Spanish bluebells (*Scilla hispanica*)

decaying leaves from oaks in particular. Rhododendrons and
azaleas seem to prefer natural acidifiers rather than chemical
compounds.

DRAINAGE

Drainage is the proper drawing off of excess water from
the soil, and is an extremely important factor in the well-
being of plants. This happens naturally when the subsoil
is not so dense as to be almost hard pan. When the water

20

cannot drain through the earth, it dilutes the soil nutriment. It also prevents the roots from stretching down into the earth, forcing them to develop surface rootage which dries out quickly when drought comes. It is also possible for drainage to be too sharp, which results in the washing away of much nutriment and the quick drying out of the soil. To create good drainage the soil may be removed to a depth greater than that required for planting, the lower portion of the hole then being filled with rocks, sand, gravel, ashes, or anything which will absorb excess moisture. If necessary a drain may be installed of unglazed tile two to five inches in diameter. These would generally be laid in a trench two or three feet deep. The tiles should slope very slightly toward the outlet, perhaps a three-inch pitch to a fifty-foot length. If there is no brook or no sewage system into which the water might flow, a hole may be dug several feet deeper than the line of tile and two or more feet wide. This dry well is then filled with stones, and earth may be laid over the surface.

Foes and Friends in the Garden

THE GARDENER'S ENEMIES

The best regulated gardens are not immune to occasional attacks from insects and diseases. No matter how carefully we tend our gardens, there is no accounting for the tastes and fancies of the insects, though most of them have their definite preferences. Nor can we foretell what tricks the atmosphere may play upon the well-being of even reputedly trouble-free plants. Yet the number of consistently immune kinds of plants is unfortunately few. Though we are not troublemongers it is well to be prepared.

Briefly, there are two main classifications of insects—those which chew holes, and those which suck juices from stem, stalk, leaf and flower. The chewers are primarily worms, beetles and grasshoppers. Also among the chewing insects are borers and leaf miners which work inside the plant tissues and are difficult to detect and to destroy. The suckers are mealy bugs, thrips, leaf hoppers, aphids, scale insects, red spider and other almost invisible mites.

To destroy chewing insects we must thoroughly spray or dust the leaves and flowers upon which they feed with a remedy which will poison their stomachs. The sucking insects are killed when we paralyze their respirative operations by a direct contact dust or spray. The third scourge is disease such as black spot, mildew or other fungus and bacterial infections. Plants are even subject to virus organisms.

Those who believe in preparedness will have a plant medicine chest where the garden tools are lined up. Near by there will no doubt be a spray gun and a pistol duster. Excellent general purpose remedies are to be had from dealers in garden supplies. The insecticide-fungicide combination dusts are especially easy to use, and they require no mixing with water as is necessary when using a spray. For very small gardens or for indoor gardening push-button bombs are easy and effective.

I do not mean to imply that plant pathology can be tossed off in too simple a manner, for one remedy could scarcely be a cure-all. Those who are baffled by unidentifiable troubles may wisely communicate with their county agricultural agent or state experiment station, either of which will give them free advice, and so will the botanical garden experts. The garden page editors of the newspapers will answer written questions. Almost every state has a garden center where advice may be had. The government Department of Agriculture will send bulletins on a great variety of subjects. Nurserymen and seedsmen will help. Consult if you will a good garden encyclopaedia or manual.

THE GARDENER'S FRIENDS AND HELPERS

The handsome moth you see flitting about your garden may in his youth have been that worm which ate up your plants. But—there are some garden insects which are truly our friends. They help to destroy grubs, larvae, etc., which are destructive in our gardens. Among the good garden helpers is the ladybug in all its incarnations. Then there is the praying mantis, with his bulging eyes and grasshopper-like legs. The dragonfly, the toad, and the wasp are useful also. Even the mole, though definitely on the debit side on account of his burrowings, has to his credit the destruction of hordes of insects in the form of grubs. The great flat, shiny black beetle which hides under rocks is a great caterpillar hunter. That drab-colored creature which looks like an overgrown and slightly weary horsefly works good deeds for us too. And the birds—how they raise havoc in the insect world. Who is champion insect catcher—chickadee or robin?

3

PLANTING AND MAINTAINING THE SHADED GARDEN

It is said that those who do not raise their own flowers from seed are really not gardeners at all. With this I would not agree. It is true that one takes extraordinary interest in plants one has raised oneself—and the garden funds stretch farther. To buy seedlings may be a costly matter, but an enormous amount of time and energy may thus be preserved and used in other directions. I once bought a packet of mixed wild flower seeds and broadcast them in our woodland. I didn't even look to see what seeds were included in the mixture—I thought it more fun to be surprised. In my ignorance I did not know that seeds are not scattered just "hit or miss." It is true that nature does this, but the casualties are tremendous. Well—I waited—and had my surprise, for a golden-glow sprang up in the violet patch.

Perhaps the best time to plant perennial seeds is in early summer in order that they may make good growth and be transplanted by autumn into permanent position, where many of them will bloom the following year. But some perennials take more time to flower and will not bloom for two or three years after the seeds are sown, as for example globe-flower (Trollius) and Christmas-rose (Helleborus).

Whether to set out perennial seedlings in spring or fall is still a moot point. In autumn the earth may be more easily worked because it is less soggy. There may be more leisure at that time, for spring activities come with a great rush. Yet, with fall planting the seedlings may not have acquired hardiness to withstand a very severe winter, and they may also be heaved up by alternate freezing and thawing. Very early bloomers may well be set out in autumn, as for example, bleeding-heart, early kinds of anemone, hepatica, early phlox and primrose. Trillium is best moved when in bloom or immediately after. Iris should be moved soon after it has ceased blooming, and spring bulbs of course are planted in autumn. Very late bloomers like Japanese anemone are best planted in spring. The planting of shrubs is generally considered most satisfactory when done in the spring, especially the evergreens.

In shade gardening it is preferable to leave more space between plants than would be necessary in the sunny garden. To make up in part for lack of sun, plants should have additional breathing space. In border planting, several of the same plants may be grouped together, say three to nine according to their size and spread and the amount of space allotted. One must bear in mind probable increase. Some plants like monkshood will not increase, or only very slowly, while phlox, day-lilies, many of the spring bulbs and a host of other plants increase rapidly. Most perennials may be counted upon to increase somewhat at least.

The importance of deep preparation of the soil cannot be overemphasized. The perennial bed should be dug from one to two feet deep, and prepared with utmost care, for the plants are going to remain there for some time, and a good beginning is well worth the effort.

There is no economy in trying to doctor a heavy clay soil or an alkaline soil when planting the acid-loving Ericaceae (rhododendron, laurel and others in this category, see page 110). It had best be dug out to the necessary depth and replaced with the correct kind of soil. Good drainage will be necessary, and to insure success the bed can be prepared with acid woods soil. Good porous garden soil will do if rendered acid. These plants should be continually moist, but well drained. All the year round they should have a mulch of pine needles or oak leaves, but not beech or maple, for these pack down too tight and do not permit the plants to breathe. Because the roots are so near the surface, stirring up the earth may injure these ericaceous plants, so it is better not to cultivate. If planted too near a plaster or cement wall they may suffer from alkalinity caused by rainwater which, as it runs down the walls, carries with it dissolved calcium. For these and other evergreens, a good soaking of the ground before frost is beneficial, for winter drought often proves very harmful.

Because shade in its variations is the theme of this book, the gardener is urged to consider cautiously the spots which are to be planted. It would be well to plan this when the trees are in full leaf, in order to know how much shade to expect. Late summer planting may then be done, or the situation noted and the planting held over until spring. Planting under trees of densest foliage should be given careful consideration, nor should planting be carried out under trees which have too many surface roots. This can easily be determined by simply digging and finding out the facts! Periodic root pruning may be done, but not too drastically. To decrease the heavy shade under trees, limb and branch pruning are permissible, and the work should be done preferably by an expert.

If plants content in half shade had their say, the majority of them would I believe prefer to be shaded during the middle part of the day when the sun is hottest. Even plants which demand almost full sun would appreciate a little shelter at noon.

Perennials in the wild garden will want some sort of cover of dead leaves, for in a woodland association that is what nature would give them, and for winter protection one can do no better than watch just what nature does. For the first season the plants should not be allowed to dry out, but when once established they will, if properly planted, take care of themselves. If plenty of space surrounds them they will not immediately be crowded out by rampant woodland growths. In the spring, heavy mats of wet leaves may have to be removed if they interfere with the freedom of certain fragile plants, but as a rule woodland plants will take fairly good care of themselves. During the growing season a little cultivation and mulching with a mixture of sand and leaf mould would be welcome. It is pleasant to make tours of inspection and give to these plants the helping hand they may require, especially those along the path.

In the formalized garden of lawns, beds and borders, near pools and among rocks, where horticultural varieties, hybrids and sophisticated plantings abound, a general clearing up will of course be wanted, for continuous good grooming is here essential. Good friable earth will be needed where frost and winter ravages have played havoc. Litter will of course be removed and the ground cultivated and fertilized if necessary. The maintenance does not differ much from that in any garden in the sun. Where there is much root

An all-over pattern of trilliums and primroses

interference more water and plant nutrients are necessary, otherwise a shade garden requires no especial handling— less watering where the sun does not dry out the soil, and less weeding, for which we are grateful.

There are plants which are finicky and there are those which need coddling, but there is a difference in the application of those two words. In the first category are those which do well and are perfectly happy if given their proper cultural requirements. Plants like creeping snowberry (Chiogenes) are finicky because they absolutely demand an acid soil. Plants in the second class are those which are for some reason difficult to raise and hard to please, as for example, some of the fringed orchis and fringed polygala. (Has the fringe anything to do with it?) In that class I also place those plants which are hardy only if protected in winter. It scarcely seems fair to subject a plant to conditions to which it is temperamentally unsuited. How lovely is the glossy-leaved English holly—but few can grow it successfully even as far north as New York City. I for one would not encase an ancient box hedge in scaffolding and burlap, or wrap the tenderlings in a plastic sheet. I'm afraid it is not kindness of heart which forbids, but purely æsthetic motives. One thing I would always do, and that is be very extravagant with the purchase of Christmas greens (the approved kinds). I could scarcely wait for the Christmas holidays to be over so that I might dismantle the tree and remove wreath and bough and drag them out of doors before they withered. I would lay them, like tributes, over all the plants which needed an extra cover. This serves not so much as winter protection from cold as protection from sun. An advantage to gardening in the shade is that plants are thus protected from winter sunburn as, for example, the mahonia or the English ivy. Shade protection is also helpful to plants which are not always hardy, like the Japanese Pieris, English holly, or box.

Most herbaceous perennials will be content without any winter covering, but some of the deciduous shrubs would appreciate a coat of old manure. The evergreens will want a mulch of leaves, especially oak leaves. Covering should not be done until after the ground is frozen (reason: mice seeking refuge do damage there). The woodland takes care of itself, gradually covering its plants gently with leaves from deciduous trees—and so winter comes.

Evergreen Christmas fern, the most useful of all

4

GARDEN TYPES

Wild Woodland and Suggested Plantings

PIONEERING IN THE TANGLE

A portion of property often remains undeveloped for years because it seems so impossible, so hopeless, one does not know what to do with it. The ground is all hills and dales and underbrush, "too much shade anyway; so of course nothing will grow." Here is not a hopeless problem, but an opportunity for expression. If one were to set about exploring this potential paradise by studying its trees and finding out "who is who," a good start would be made. Where the tangle is too dense and impossible to penetrate without tearing garment and temper, then a helper might hew a little foot-path to a given point that the lay of the land may be studied.

If, in deciduous woodland, oaks and dogwoods are present, then there may be some maple-leaved viburnum, wild honeysuckle, columbine, anemones, violets. There is definite rhyme and reason why certain trees and shrubs live in ordered association. They may benefit in one way or another by these interrelations, perhaps through shading each other, or supplying certain organic matters, etc. Seeds fly through the air and fall everywhere, but unless the surroundings are congenial, they will not grow. They may germinate and sprout, but they soon die down, incapable of coping with the conditions wrong for their well-being.

In an association where cone-bearing evergreens predominate, one will of course find shade-loving undergrowth planting, such as ferns, bunchberry (Cornus canadensis), even wild orchids—some plants in dry spots, others in moist ones. Influenced by certain ecological factors, this wild garden will be designed after Nature, and hers is a pretty good pattern.

We may see a woodland flower in bloom and neglect to mark the spot, but we remember its foliage. Later in the season the plant has disappeared, its leaves having vanished. There are certain plants whose nature it is to begin losing their foliage after flowering. Among these are:

Claytonia
(spring beauty)

Dentaria
(toothwort)

Dicentra cucullaria
(Dutchman's-breeches)

Erythronium
(trout-lily)

Maianthemum
(Canada mayflower)

Mertensia
(Virginia bluebell)

Sanguinaria
(blood-root)

Ornithogalum
(star-of-Bethlehem)

It might be well to study carefully, for a season, the locality where a garden is to be built, to see what happens naturally. Put in stakes where the treasures are, and pluck specimens of flower and leaf to match them up with illustrations and text of an authoritative plant manual, of which

Invitation to the wild garden

there are so many. In this way one may take stock of material already at hand, and pleasantly learn a great deal. If one is already familiar with plant nomenclature, so much the better. First we love our woodland, then we are eager to work for it, and soon we reap our reward.

This tract then is to be developed as a wooded wild garden. What exactly is a wild garden? It is one in which Nature appears to have done all the landscape planning unaided. It does not mean that this garden should contain native material exclusively. Why limit oneself, when the whole world is there from which to make a choice? There is no reason why a few foreigners from Europe and the Far East should not find a place in this garden, provided they are hardy and can be given their accustomed and appropriate surroundings. Many plants, like people, have become naturalized in this country, as for instance certain primroses, narcissus, hesperis, sweet woodruff and forget-me-not. However, going completely native will certainly not cramp our freedom, for our own vast flora allows us abundant choice. If it is known that certain Rocky Mountain wildings will grow and prosper in the East under similar conditions of soil, situation, and shade as in their native habitat, then again there is no reason why we should not let them colonize in New England or any other suitable locality. There are many plants which botanists tell us have escaped from cultivation. How amusing it is to think of them as scampering off to the woods, where in slightly touseled form they thrive as contented savages!

The best way to create a wild garden is, of course, to observe how the wild things actually grow in relation to their surroundings. To naturalize a group of plants in a wild garden means to establish them there, where they will take care of themselves, once they have become acclimated. In clearing spots in the woodland where plantings are to be made, it is well to study the locality at the height of its summer growth to determine how much space to clear away, always allowing sufficient for plant increase. If the plants spread by leaps and bounds, more space may be cleared later. There is no reason why great clearings should be made, as it might take years for the new colony to take possession.

Of all types, the wild garden is the least troublesome to maintain, assuming of course that one has done his utmost to meet all the planting requirements. Plants will naturally need looking after, but they will not demand the meticulous grooming which is so necessary in a formalized garden.

Some plants, like trailing arbutus, insist definitely upon intensely acid soil. And where is that to be found? In porous soil, often among oaks and evergreens. He who sets his heart upon planting this fastidious gem must be sure of the soil reaction, for that seems to be its principal idiosyncrasy, and yet arbutus is not easily satisfied.

If the topographical contours of the proposed wild garden are irregular, the planting may be more varied and effective than if the ground were level. Still more opportunities will present themselves if one is so fortunate as to have a stream where moisture affords hospitality to lush growth, while pockets in rocky ledges are rosetted with maidenhair spleenworts and their associates.

In opening up the woodland to give light and breathing

space to fine, promising trees, it is essential to know that where there are waterways, trees should be preserved, lest, by their removal, the waters dry away. Many a well-meaning gardener has too late discovered this fact, with all his plans for planting the stream-side thwarted.

Unless one is familiar with the good and bad habits of trees, it would be well to call into consultation a tree expert, who may advise which trees have the greatest value and which should be eliminated. For example, if one were to choose between an American linden and a white oak, admitting that they both have beauty, the former would be discarded because its branches are more easily broken by winds, and because of its susceptibility to borers.

Surely everyone agrees that there is no more satisfactory tree the year round than flowering dogwood. Study its seasonal habits and note the petals, properly bracts, as they unfold—sulphur yellow at first. To see a pair of scarlet tanagers alight at this time is a radiant sight indeed. This tree starts the autumn season by being among the first to turn color, matching its lovely red berry clusters. If in your tree association there exists a spindly forest of dogwood saplings, it is far better that some be eliminated to allow each remaining one sufficient space in which to develop. This would of course be true with any plant material.

If shade in the woodland is too deep in certain spots, branches and even limbs as previously stated may be removed with skillful handling, but obviously too much amputation at one time would have its ruinous effects. Probably certain of the maples and hornbeams would lose character if their lower branches were removed, nor is it

TOP. White-flowered bloodroot (*Sanguinaria*) in early spring

BOTTOM. A carpet of bunchberries (*Cornus canadensis*)

usually advisable to take away the lower limbs of conifers in order to show their trunks. Dead branches will of course be cut away, and so will the limbs which cross one another and interfere with the tree's beauty of structure.

In pioneering in the tangle much underbrush will undoubtedly be found, clutters of thorny vines and weedy shrubs. These may be carefully grubbed out to reveal stately tree trunks and the dark woodland floor. With confusion removed, one begins to visualize a new and more alluring composition of potential materials.

Rocks with any character should be retained, especially those of ruggedness and interesting color. They create a delightful background, and are the natural environment for a great many woodland plants.

A path system may then be planned, a meandering ribbon skirting proposed spots of both permanent and seasonal interest. In March, we look for the first signs of life—the silver maple, the pussy willow, skunk-cabbage, hepatica, rue-anemone. Visualize a great waving colony of spring beauty on the sunny hillside, near a grove of naked oaks, whose myriad branchlets produce fine shadows upon the warming earth. Is not that worth going to see? Somewhat later, in a sheltered and rocky ledge we find the first bloodroot in flower, the stem of each white blossom wrapped separately in its own silver leaf, cornucopia-wise. The Indians knew this little plant and used the juice of stem and root as a dye for their skin.

Week by week in winding down the wildwood path there is something new and surprising, for often one forgets just what is due to bloom next. Except for a periodic outburst of drama, a garden of this character is peaceful on the whole with its green and brown predominant notes. One comes casually upon blooming things, carefully planned for careless effect. For weight and interest away from the path, are planted groups of deciduous shrubs, which flower or fruit in their season. At strategic points are placed needle-leaved evergreens such as the noble hemlock and the wild American yew. With broad leaves, there are native rhododendrons and laurel, forever beautiful in flower or in leaf. Plant them in groups; they are happier so. Of these two, mountain-laurel stands up better in severely cold weather, for it keeps its leaves bravely unfurled and does not roll them up lengthwise and shiver in the cold as the rhododendron so often does.

If through the system of paths one is enabled to wander far, a short-cut home should be arranged for our convenience. When the grounds are on more than one level, a series of crude steps will be useful, and thus is created added opportunity for casual planting along the bank, beside the steps and in all the little crevices.

WOODLAND STREAM-SIDE

In Full Shade. Through a grove of evergreens and oaks, where the soil is moist and acid, a stream winds its way. A hoary hemlock droops over the embankment and near it the downy pinxter azalea, in flower, exudes a spicy perfume. It is spring and many little moisture-loving wildlings are in bloom. Where the ground yew grows, yellow lady-slippers appear from the brown earth, and near by, beneath a painted trillium, bunchberry spreads its glossy leaves. Ferns uncoil their fronds (cinnamon and giant woodfern like this spot); and the decorative royal fern, near a clump of oaks, is actually standing in shallow water, where its pink and yellow crosiers are reflected.

In June, the small lily-like flowers of Clintonia will bloom against a background of tall ferns and catawba rhododendrons. In July, the fragrant white swamp azalea bursts forth intertwined with still more ferns, while birds wait for blueberries to ripen. Wood-sorrel in its delicate beauty of trefoil leaf is here among rocks at the water's edge, and beyond is a carpet of galax with shining round leaves. In the mossy waterside, where sunshine filters through for several hours a day, the twin-flower trails its evergreen leaves from which pink flowers spring on tiny stalks from May to August.

In Light Shade. The stream flows on, the woodland grows brighter, for we have left the evergreen belt, but the soil is still moist, though on the whole less acid.

Here we find among the rocks at the stream-side, mertensia, pink and blue, in May; and with some ostrich ferns is jack-in-the-pulpit. Spice-bush bloomed early and clethra is soon to bud.

From May through July, in light woodland we have, blooming in their turn, the lovely native orchids (Orchis and Habenaria) in moisture among the stones. Grouped in the background are some hobble-bushes, while light and sunshine penetrate a little more. Delicate forget-me-nots bloom in spots along the stream's edge, and wild mint perfumes the air.

In July and August, a great splash of red brightens the thin woodland in that moist spot across the stream—the brilliant cardinal-flower.

Half Shade. The stream bed grows wider, and the sun's rays now play for half a day as the season advances. But while the marsh-marigold blooms, the deciduous trees are still quite bare. Presently the large blue flag appears among ferns, and later the yellow meadow lily with tall meadow-rue.

Atop the bank, as the season wanes and autumn approaches, there are various members of the dogwood family, viburnums and sassafras, all in flaming autumn dress. Below them grows a swaying mass of Christmas-ferns. Clustered beyond near the water are closed gentians, exclusive and very blue, of which Donald Culross Peattie writes so delightfully:

"Of all colors, a gentian's blue is the favorite of the bees; it would seem a flower preëminently attractive to those melliferous matchmakers. Yet this gentian never admits the bee, nor the long-tongued moth or butterfly; perpetually the great blue bottles remain corked. Within, a perfect mechanism insures self-fertilization—perhaps a lucky circumstance for a flower that blooms when frosts are nigh. They bloom secretive, remote, sufficient to themselves—flowers with a sad dignity, offerings upon the grave of the year."*

* Donald Culross Peattie: *An Almanac for Moderns*; G. P. Putnam's Sons; New York; 1935.

RIGHT. Ferns uncoil their fronds.

RÉSUMÉ OF PLANT MATERIAL IN THE PRECEDING SECTION

WOODLAND STREAM-SIDE

The shade ranges from deep to half shade, in evergreen and in deciduous woodland. All the plants below revel in moisture, but many of them are just as happy in other situations.

Evergreens

Kalmia latifolia
    (mountain-laurel)
Rhododendron catawbiense
    (catawba rhododendron)

Taxus canadensis
    (American yew)
Tsuga canadensis
    (hemlock)

Deciduous Shrubs

Azalea rosea
    (downy pinxterbloom)
Azalea viscosa
    (white swamp azalea)
Lindera benzoin
    (spice-bush)

Clethra alnifolia
    (summer sweet)
Cornus in variety
    (dogwood)
Vaccinium species
    (blueberry)

Viburnum alnifolium (hobble-bush)

Ferns

Osmunda cinnamomea
    (cinnamon-fern)
Dryopteris goldiana
    (giant woodfern)

Osmunda regalis
    (royal-fern)
Polystichum acrostichoides
    (Christmas-fern)

Pteretis nodulosa (ostrich-fern)

Perennials

Arisæma triphyllum
(jack-in-the-pulpit)

Caltha palustris
(marsh-marigold)

Clintonia borealis
(blue-bead)

Cornus canadensis
(bunchberry)

Cypripedium calceolus
(yellow lady-slipper)

Galax aphylla
(galax)

Gentian andrewsii
(closed gentian)

Habenaria blephariglottis
(white fringed orchis)

Habenaria ciliaris
(yellow fringed orchis)

Habenaria psycodes
(large purple fringed orchis)

Iris versicolor
(blue flag)

Lilium canadense
(meadow lily)

Linnæa borealis
(twin-flower)

Lobelia cardinalis
(cardinal-flower)

Mentha arvensis
(wild mint)

Mertensia virginica
(virginia bluebell)

Myosotis scorpioides
(forget-me-not)

Orchis spectabilis
(showy orchis)

Oxalis montana
(wood-sorrel)

Trillium undulatum
(painted trillium)

THE SHADED POND

A Setting for Plants Which Like Moist Soil. At sunset in earliest spring the golden osier willows grouped at the water's edge appear like fountains playing in golden light. Near by, on the bank among rocks, are splashes of yellow marsh marigolds, and then a group of silvery birches glisten in the moonlight.

The red and black chokeberries bloom white in May, and the red-osier dogwood too is in flower. In June some handsome viburnums flourish in the moist soil by the pond's side. A little later the wild hydrangea sends forth its striking heads of white flowers.

At the water's edge in light shade is the tall solomons-seal, and in half shade the variegated sweet flag creates a pleasant vertical note. The water surface is strewn in a charming pattern with floating-heart. Lizards-tail stands in water, and in the lightest spots, blue flag.

In June and July we see spires of astilbe, in casual masses with feathery cream-color bloom, and groups of tawny day-lilies all in half shade.

What is that fascinating plant over there across the pond with huge indented leaves and subtropical effect? It's a foreigner from the Caucasus, and it must be ten feet high! That is giant cow-parsnip, placed there strategically against a dark background of green, to bring into relief its gigantic white flower heads.

Many plants blossom here at the waterside in July and August. The orange turks-cap lily in half shade, and the meadow lily in reds and yellows of brilliant hue, and spikes of white turtle-heads with their pinkish "lips." Under the poplars and white birches the tall ostrich-ferns make plume-like harmony, and in the distance red bee-balm is aflame.

In September the fields are gay with bright blue-violet New York asters. But there is more to enjoy—the brilliancy of autumn leaf and the berries—red, white, blue and black —of dogwood, viburnum, and chokeberry.

RÉSUMÉ OF PLANT MATERIAL IN THE PRECEDING SECTION

RANGING FROM LIGHT SHADE TO HALF SHADE

The Shaded Pond

Shrubs

Aronia arbutifolia
  (red chokeberry)

Aronia melanocarpa
  (black chokeberry)

Cornus stolonifera
  (red-osier dogwood)

Hydrangea arborescens
  (smooth hydrangea)

Viburnum cassinoides (withe rod)

Perennials

Aster novi-belgii
  (New York aster)

Astilbe species
  (false spirea)

Caltha palustris
  (marsh-marigold)

Chelone glabra
  (turtle-head)

Hemerocallis fulva
  (tawny day-lily)

Heracleum villosum
  (cow-parsnip)

Lilium canadense
  (meadow lily)

Lilium superbum
  (turks-cap lily)

Monarda didyma
  (bee-balm)

Polygonatum commutatum
  (solomons-seal)

Aquatics

Acorus calamus (sweet flag)   Iris versicolor (blue flag)

Saururus cernuus (lizards-tail)

Fern

Pteretis nodulosa (ostrich-fern)

GROTESQUES

What are those weird signs of life on the woodland floor in earliest spring, those strange outcroppings among the sere brown leaves in moist low spots? Skunk cabbage in embryo! Soon the whole locality will burst forth with absurd green tufts, and once more the woodland comes into its renaissance.

Garden gargoyles lend humor to Nature's propriety. In free spots which are wild and unpruned let us leave undisturbed those touches which amuse us as we pass them by. Have we a tree whose form bends and twists into strange patterns, or a gnome of the forest? Let us humor it and give it a place of honor.

A gnarled old vine which reaches up into the topmost branches of some tree in our woodland garden may produce neither blossom, berry nor interesting leaf, yet it has woven itself into wild tracery, like rusty iron-work with curlicue and spiral gone mad! Keep it and be intrigued by its mystery, especially in moonlight. There is so much of interest in common things. Take the big pine cones, the nut burs and seed pods, and observe how Nature improvised, long ago, and then cut her patterns—with tongue in cheek!

Let us not hastily tear down and uproot strange growths, which in early spring seem to hold no promise. On the sunny fringe of a dense forest in Japan I once saw, clambering up into the tall trunked evergreens, a vast expanse of wild tangled vine, like a fantastic openwork curtain screening the woodland. Two months later, passing that same spot and remembering, I looked again to see my vine now come to life, festooning the pines, all dripping with purple wisteria in ripe bloom.

Little drifts of toadstools, now we see them, now we don't. Pert, illusive things which pop up after the rains, and disintegrate as quickly as they came. They are brilliant, they are drab, some with pebbly domes, others of long legs and rakish tops—orange, fawn, gold, pink and speckled ones too. And what of the varied fungus strata, colorful excrescences which break out on trees?

Then the mosses, a study in themselves, strange texture and stranger forms. They are called by such fitting names as fairy cups, sponges, pincushions, knights-plumes and old-mans-beard. And lichens in weird blotches sit upon rocks and on trees, like frost crystals in cold color.

The surface rootwork of a grand old tree may trace a vigorous pattern, octopus-like. I have seen, and so have you, tree trunks whose bark had wrinkled itself into tiers of comic faces almost like weathered totem poles, with a gray-green patch of lichen where a phantom eye should be.

Draw aside the lower branches of an ancient evergreen, and there stands a ghoulish group of indian-pipes, like frozen wax, ghostly white. Gargoyles!

Formalized Garden of Beds and Borders

The word formalized is used here to signify all types of gardens of form and pattern, as distinguished from the wild garden, where the semblance of studied design is avoided.

It is hoped that the gardener not interested in wild gardening will nevertheless read that chapter, for in it there is

scarcely a plant mentioned which is unsuited to the cultivated garden. Many old favorites are there, such as orchids,
columbine, snakeroot, lobelia, and most of these wildlings
improve enormously when given the comforts of a well-
ordered garden. As for shrubs, the woodland produces its
aristocrats too.

Of course no one will want in the border a row of Jack-
in-the-pulpit, but why not under a great spreading tree a
group of ferns with one Jack among them? No one wants
amidst his fragile flowers, like bluebells and wild geranium,
a restless bedfellow like bee-balm, which grabs all the space.
One can imagine, though, in some rough spot, bee-balm fill-
ing the vacancy and flourishing en masse. Its value lies in its
scarlet flowers in midsummer shade. Who wants in his
modest-size garden a giant cow-parsnip, with flowers the
size of cauliflower heads? The thought is absurd, but on
spacious grounds, in just the right setting, this dramatic
monster has its place. And what of giant butter-bur with
leaves the size of the ears of an elephant? Excellent for sub-
tropical effect, if in the right location. Material on a small
scale for the small garden—but on vast grounds there is
space for limitless expression.

There are many plants mentioned in the chapter on wild
gardening which will fit appropriately in the well-groomed
rock garden—hepatica—gentian—lady-slipper—violet. Consider all the wild orange and yellow lilies among tall trees,
and wild iris near the shaded pool, and some astilbe in
the border. For edging isn't forget-me-not a good subject?
Though of foreign ancestry it seems happy enough naturalized here in the wild. If a long blooming season is desired,

the variety semperflorens is recommended for the cultivated garden.

If I could stimulate an interest in the greater appreciation
of ferns, I should feel that this book had justified its exist-
ence. People often speak disparagingly about ferns because
they are just "greens." Think of the range of color in those
greens. Contrast the deep fronds of evergreen Christmas-
ferns and delicate spleenworts with the pale fronds of male
and hay-scented-ferns. Note the gloss on ground-cedar as
it lies sprawling among rocks. Compare the textures of
maidenhair-fern with any of these. Note the urn-like silhou-
ette of the ostrich-fern, and the majesty of giant woodfern.
Yes, there is plenty of color, for doesn't the royal fern have
beautiful yellow and pink crosiers and henna seed pods, and
doesn't the rattlesnake fern, flushed rose and mulberry,
have a cluster of chartreuse "fruits" in late spring? With
what fascination do we observe the little walking fern which
produces its offspring at the tip of a frond which bends to
the earth that the new plant may root there. But it refuses
to "walk" unless in congenial environment. Ferns are
tolerant as a rule of many situations, but for the best results,
their native soil beds should be more or less reproduced in
the garden. As shade is here our chief concern, ferns are its
most valued allies.

Wild plants, we find, then, are suitable to the cultivated
garden, but we cannot say the reverse. It is not only hazard-
ous but inappropriate to plant highly civilized horticultural
varieties in the wild. Hybridizers do a noble work in the
interest of gardening, but Nature does some on her own
too. Consider, for example, the violets with all their wild

intermarrying. Sometimes even the botanist is bewildered.

You would certainly not plant a tuberous-rooted begonia in a wild garden, nor would you want there a tea rose, even though you could give them the proper culture. How lovely a shaded bed on a flagstone terrace would be filled with begonia evansiana. Its pink blooms are effective, and in a sheltered place the plant would probably winter, for this is the only hardy begonia for our temperate gardens. However, tuberous begonias in their marvelous forms and colorings should not be overlooked as shade candidates.

The question of planting near the roots of trees bears consideration in gardening in the shade. Beware of maples, beech, sycamore, because their root systems are so near the surface of the soil, and, as mentioned before, they absorb an enormous amount of moisture and nourishment. The Norway maple is notorious on this account. I have seldom seen anything grow successfully under this tree. The density of its foliage is also to be taken into account, for it creates a heavy shade. Unless one were willing to go to the trouble of constant feeding and watering one had better plant else-where. The most that may be hoped is that English ivy, periwinkle, pachysandra, or creeping Charlie (Lysimachia) might oblige, but probably even those useful and desirable plants will need periodic encouragement. Veronica officinalis sometimes does well in obstinate dark corners. Carpet bugle might comply, goutweed (Aegopodium) would do it, if not allowed to invade lawn or border.

The gardener who plants in the shade must consider a number of factors before deciding upon the correct location of his beds. He should consider (1) the amount and the density of shade at all times, (2) tree-root interference, and (3) the possibility of too much drip from trees. House leaders with improper underground drainage, leaky roofs and awnings come under this category as well. We in America are not troubled by this condition as seriously as the English are, because we have less moisture. It is well, when planting, to avoid a situation which may drown or crush small delicate plants. Neither are large plants immune, for even shrubs are sometimes seriously damaged by this condition. Moisture-loving plants may thrive near a puddle, yet I doubt if they would care for a gush of rain-water on their heads.

The golden marsh-marigold thrives in moisture.

SUGGESTED PLANTINGS FOR THE FORMALIZED GARDEN

FOUNDATION PLANTING ON THE NORTH SIDE OF A HOUSE OR WALL OR WHERE THERE IS ALMOST CONTINUOUS SHADE

See also section on ground covers, page 115

Non-Flowering Evergreens

Euonymus fortunei, shrub or climbing forms

Ilex crenata (Japanese holly) and its forms

Taxus (yew) several species and varieties

Tsuga (hemlock) will in time reach high and broad proportions

Christmas-fern, evergreen wood-fern, others

Flowering Evergreens

They may not bloom profusely, but they are none the less handsome in foliage.

Azalea. Many kinds both ever-green and not

Kalmia latifolia (mountain-laurel)

Leucothoë catesbaei

Pieris floribunda and P. Japonica (andromeda)

Rhododendron species and hy-brids

FRAGRANCE IN THE SHADE

Shrubs

Azalea, several species

Calycanthus (sweet-shrub)

Clematis, several species

Daphne cneorum (garland flower)

Daphne mezereum (February daphne)

Lonicera, several species

Philadelphus (mock-orange)

Wisteria, Chinese white variety

Rose, many kinds

Symplocos (Asiatic sweetleaf)

Perennials

Convallaria (lily-of-the-valley)

Epigaea (trailing arbutus)

Hemerocallis (day-lilies) many
  kinds

Hesperis (dames-rocket)

Hosta plantaginea
  (fragrant plantain-lily)

Lilium hansonii (Hanson's lily)

Lilium regale (regal lily)

Narcissus, many kinds

Phlox paniculata
  (summer perennial phlox)

Valeriana (common valerian)

Viola odorata
  (sweet garden violets in
  masses)

THE ROCK GARDEN IN FULL SHADE

(Those plants marked with an * demand special soil conditions.
See Part Two, "Who's Who in the Shade")

Spring

Ajuga (bugle)

*Coptis (goldthread)

*Cornus canadensis
  (bunchberry)

*Cypripedium acaule
  (pink lady-slipper)

*Epigæa (trailing arbutus)

Iris verna (dwarf iris) and Iris
  cristata (crested iris)

Orchis spectabilis
  (showy orchis)

*Oxalis montana
  (American wood-sorrel)

*Polygala

Sanguinaria (bloodroot)

Scilla hispanica
  (Spanish bluebell)

Sedum ternatum

*Shortia (oconee-bells)

Trientalis (starflower)

Trillium

Viola, several species

Summer

*Chimaphila (pipsissewa)

*Clintonia (blue-bead)

Dalibarda

Dicentra eximia
    (fringed bleeding-heart)

Galax

*Gaultheria (wintergreen)

Goodyera (rattlesnake plantain)

Hosta (plantain-lily or funkia),
    small leaf forms

*Linnæa (twin-flower)

Mimulus moschatus
    (musk plant)

*Pyrola (shinleaf)

A pleasant combination of ferns and bugle (*Ajuga*) which care for themselves

LIGHT SHADE IN THE BORDER

FRONT BORDER	MIDDLE BORDER	REAR BORDER

Spring

FRONT BORDER	MIDDLE BORDER	REAR BORDER

Ajuga (bugle)
Asperula
(sweet woodruff)
Epimedium
(barrenwort)
Myosotis scorpioides
  semperflorens
(forget-me-not)
Omphalodes verna
(creeping forget-me-not)
Pulmonaria (lungwort)
Vancouveria
(American barrenwort)
Spring bulbs, especially
  Scilla
	Dicentra spectabilis
	(bleeding-heart)
	Mertensia
	(Virginia bluebell)
		Shrubs may partially fill
		this space but they must
		not interfere with the
		plants which bloom later
		in the rear border.

Summer

FRONT BORDER	MIDDLE BORDER	REAR BORDER
Chrysogonum (golden-star) *Dicentra eximia* (fringed bleeding-heart) *Hosta* (small varieties) (plantain-lily) *Myosotis scorpioides* *semperflorens* (forget-me-not)	*Aconitum napellus* (true monkshood) *Buphthalmum* (showy ox-eye) *Campanula latifolia* (great bellflower) *Digitalis purpurea* (common foxglove) *Filipendula* (meadow-sweet)	*Cimicifuga racemosa* (black snakeroot) *Hemerocallis* (day-lily) *Hypericum prolificum* (shrubby St. Johnswort) *Thalictrum dipterocarpum* (meadow-rue)

LIGHT SHADE IN THE BORDER

FRONT BORDER	MIDDLE BORDER	REAR BORDER

Summer

FRONT BORDER	MIDDLE BORDER	REAR BORDER
Begonia (tuberous B.) in strong light almost no sun *Begonia semperflorens* (wax B.) in sun or light shade *Ceratostigma* (plumbago)	*Hemerocallis* (day-lily) *Hesperis* (dames-rocket) *Hosta* (plantain-lily) *Hypericum calycinum* (St. Johnswort) *Ligularia clivorum* *Lilium tigrinum* (tiger lily) *Physostegia virginiana* (false dragonhead) *Platycodon grandiflorum* (balloon-flower) *Primula japonica* (Japanese primrose) *Thalictrum delavayi* (meadow-rue) *Thalictrum flavum* (meadow-rue)	See previous page under Summer

Autumn

FRONT BORDER	MIDDLE BORDER	REAR BORDER
	Anemone japonica (Japanese anemone) *Cimicifuga simplex* (black snakeroot) *Eupatorium rugosum* (white snakeroot) *Hemerocallis* (day-lily) *Hosta* (plantain-lily)	*Aconitum fischeri* *Aconitum uncinatum* (wild monkshood) *Hemerocallis* (day-lily) *Senecio tanguticus*

A FEW COLOR HARMONIES IN VARYING DEGREES OF SHADE

Spring

Daphne mezereum and Chionodoxa (glory-of-the-snow)
Tiny spring bulbs, blue, pink or white beneath the purple blossoms on naked stems of Daphne.

Ceris canadensis (redbud or judas tree) and Muscari (grape hyacinth) or Ajuga (bugle)
The reddish buds and deep pink flowers of a shrubby redbud, under which are grouped blue grape hyacinths or Ajuga.

Scilla hispanica (Spanish bluebell) and maidenhair-fern
The blossoming bulbs in blue, pink and white blend with delicate young pinkish fern fronds. Later when the bulb leaves turn yellow, the mature ferns cover them.

Viola blanda, Scilla sibirica, Ornithogalum, Vinca and ferns
A bunch of sweet white violets and blue Siberian squills, a drift of white stars-of-Bethlehem, and the lavender blue of periwinkle. Christmas-ferns take over the space left bare when stars-of-Bethlehem and their foliage have disappeared.

Dicentra spectabilis, Primula vulgaris and Mertensia virginica
Rose-pink bleeding-heart, yellow primroses and Virginia bluebells, which open pink and turn lavender-blue.

Tulip kaufmanniana and Scilla sibirica
A massing of early blooming little wild (species) tulips in vivid tones of red intermingled with blue squills with their lavender cast.

Summer

Solidago (wreath goldenrod) and Lilium tigrinum (tiger lily)
Intermingling of the goldenrod with the orange or salmon-red lilies with purple spots.

Cimicifuga racemosa (black snakeroot), Hosta cærulea (plantain-lily) and Monarda fistulosa (wild bergamot)
Tall white plumes of snakeroot with the blue-lavender bells of the plantain-lily and the red-purple touselled heads of wild bergamot.

Hemerocallis and Campanula latifolia
Pale clear yellow day-lilies combined with purple-blue bellflowers.

Autumn

Aconitum wilsonii (monkshood), Cimicifuga simplex (snakeroot) and Japanese anemone
Violet monkshood, cream-white snakeroot plumes, and Japanese anemone in shades of rose.

Eupatorium cœlestinum (mist-flower) and aster novi-belgii (New York aster)
Mist-flower pom-poms and aster daisies in shades of blue-violet.

Lobelia siphilitica (blue lobelia), multiflora begonia and ferns
Lavender-blue lobelia spikes and pastel-colored begonia blossoms backed by tall ferns.

Brunnera macrophylla with Doronicum plantagineum
Blue flowers resembling forget-me-nots of Brunnera (formerly called Anchusa myosotidiflora) with the yellow daisy-like blossoms of Doronicum (leopards-bane). Both plants have coarse foliage.

Colchicum, Ceratostigma and maidenhair-ferns
A planting of ferns to mark the spot near where meadow-saffron will

emerge with its crocus-like flowers in purple, violet, rose or white. Not far away is the intense blue of plumbago.

All Season

Stachys lanata (lambs-ears), and Pulmonaria angustifolia (lungwort)
The silvery-gray leaves of lambs-ears intermingle well with the bright violet-blue flowers of Pulmonaria. Later the purple flowers of lambs-ears blend with the green and silvery leaves of both plants. The leaves remain fresh through the autumn.

Regarding Lawns in the Shade

It is almost useless to try to grow grass under densely leaved low branching trees or those with a network of surface roots. Lack of grass survival is often due not only to shade density but to malnutrition. The grass simply cannot compete for its share of food and moisture where the trees require so much.

We can of course attempt to thin or prune our trees. We can also remove those trees which serve no special purpose. Or we can, by fertilizing and watering the offending trees or shrubs, ameliorate the possibilities of lawn survival. There is always recourse to ground covers such as the faithful pachysandra, ivy, periwinkle and others discussed on pages 115-124. If none of these survives in the stubborn spots, then stone chips, pebbles, buckwheat hulls, brickwork or other appropriate paving might be preferred to bare ground.

In building a lawn the seed bed must be prepared with the utmost care as to drainage, soil texture and composition, and fertilization. If soil tests show that the pH is below 6, liming will probably be necessary.

GRASS SEEDS FOR SHADE

Red fescue (Festuca rubra) and its varieties are the standard shade grasses. They thrive in sun or shade, they even stand slightly moist soils, though dry soil is preferred, and drainage must be good. In the matter of nutriment their demands are moderate. These fescues like neutral soil but they do not object to a certain amount of acidity. They make a deep green turf of fine texture similar to Kentucky blue grass. Being somewhat wiry, they require a sharp-bladed mower set at no closer than $1\frac{1}{2}$ inches, preferably 2 inches. The most widely used fescues are the narrow-leaved ones, *i.e.* creeping red and chewing fescue.

Rough blue grass (Poa trivialis). Though inferior to the fescues, this seed is recommended for moist soils only. It should grow successfully on the north side of a building, on slopes facing north and under most shade trees. It seldom survives for any time in dry sunny areas.

"Nurse crop" *grasses.* Redtop, colonial bent or perennial rye grass are often mixed in small percentages of not over 15% to other lawn grasses. They germinate rapidly and give the new lawn a quick start while the other grasses are becoming established. These temporary grasses die out after a season or two.

There are excellent shady lawn mixtures on the market to suit most soils and conditions and the gardener is wise to buy from highly reputable houses. Quality and purity of seed is as important as the proper mixture. The presence of chaff and weedy fillers or an over-percentage of temporary grasses is to be avoided. No matter how fine the quality of seed one uses, one must not expect a perfect lawn from one sowing!

Following are a few mixtures approved for the shaded grounds:

PROPOSED SEED MIXTURES FOR DRY SHADE

75% creeping red fescue
25% Kentucky blue grass (probably the most commonly used grass in N.E. United States)

OR

70% chewing fescue
15% colonial bent (Agrostis tenuis) also called Rhode Island bent
15% redtop (Agrostis alba)

OR

In difficult spots a pure seeding of creeping red fescue alone at the rate of 7 pounds per 1000 square feet.

PROPOSED SEED MIXTURES FOR MOIST SHADE

25% creeping red fescue
25% Kentucky blue grass (Poa pretensis)
50% rough blue grass (Poa trivialis)

OR

50% chewing fescue
30% rough blue grass (Poa trivialis)
10% Kentucky blue grass
10% colonial bent

We are advised on the best authority to buy no mixture which contains tall fescue, Alta or Kentucky 31, orchard grass or meadow fescue because they are too coarse for the home ground.

The amount of seed required would vary between 2 to 5 pounds per 1000 square feet according to season and conditions.

As for fertilizers, there are many superior brands and formulas on the market. These are usually applied in early spring and again in early autumn, according to directions on the package.

Continuous Bloom in a Shaded Garden of Little Care

It is easy to have a garden in which flowers bloom from early spring until autumn. The entire project takes thought, effort and application, but once the garden is planted our work is done—or almost so for years to come. Weeding should be at a minimum, because many of the plants here included have basal ground-covering foliage.

For this easy garden we shall select fifteen kinds of plants including ferns. Flowering vines and shrubs would add immeasurably to the fullness of bloom, but let us consider here the herbaceous perennials and a few that are evergreen.

To start the pageantry of bloom we select some early spring bulbs, which, once planted, will increase and make their appearance each spring for many years without resetting or special encouragement on our part. All the bulbs here mentioned are planted in the fall. Little drifts of them are effective down the wooded path in colonies, in casual groups among rocks, in the shade of deciduous trees, in garden beds or borders and certainly where we may view them at close range from the house windows. They make pleasant patterns among ground covers and fern fronds and other appropriate plantings, which mature after the bulbs have faded and their browning foliage needs masking.

Among the earliest in spring are winter aconites (Eranthis), snowflakes (Leucojum), snowdrops (Galanthus), and glory-of-the-snow (Chionodoxa). Happily, all the bulbs to be mentioned here are seldom relished by rodents. But how they savor the gastronomic delights in a lily, a tulip and a crocus. Miniature crested iris (I. cristata) are easily contented and they increase rapidly. There will be Siberian bluebells or squills (Scilla sibirica) which resemble glory-of-the-snow but their petals appear less wind blown. Later come their taller relatives, the Spanish species (S. hispanica) and the English bluebells (S. nonscripta) but this last one has excessively large leaves which brown and wither so slowly that something must be planted to cover the ugliness, for it is essential that bulb foliage must be left to grow sere and not be cut away prematurely.

Other permanent bulbs which naturalize beautifully are grape-hyacinths (Muscari). With their tiny blue grapes they make pleasant pools of color, but white and flesh-toned ones are to be had as well. Along with these the well-beloved narcissus begin to appear, and this includes daffodils. Here our choice is great. There are single and double forms, tall and miniature, those with long trumpets or very shallow cups. We have them in pure white, through cream and yellow, with contrasting centers of vivid orange, yellow, chartreuse. Many of them become contentedly naturalized and may be left undisturbed for years in the shade of deciduous trees.

In addition to our planting of ferns among the bulbs, we add for variety some ground covers such as bugle (Ajuga), moneywort (Lysimachia nummularia), gill-over-the-ground (Nepeta hederacea) which spread mats of bloom in their season. Even without their starry blossoms, epimediums remain attractive and tidy almost into winter. Patches of lily-of-the-valley are contented, fragrant and expansive. Johnny-jump-up (Viola tricolor), which self sows, will pop up in unexpected places next and every year. Many species of violets love the shade and may be relied upon year after year. Fringed bleeding-heart (Dicentra eximia) will bloom almost all season.

As early as late April plantain-lilies (Hosta) will begin to show their young leaf shoots the size of squirrel's ears and before too long the handsome foliage matures. Then one by one a dozen plantain-lily species and varieties produce their racemes of bloom beginning in late June and continuing into late October. There are those with sensational crinkled foliage, one plant alone able, in time, to cover a space of five feet in diameter (Hosta fortunei gigantea). Some have leaves carefully bordered with white, others more white than green. Another has whorls of huge almost powder blue foliage, puckered like seersucker, but the flowers are on short scapes (H. glauca [H. sieboldiana]). There are slim leaf kinds which are comparatively dwarf (H. minor [Lancifolia var.]). The most popular of all plantain-lilies seems still to be Hosta plantaginea [H. subcordata or H. grandiflora]

No need to weed beneath the plantain-lilies

TOP. *Hosta glauca.*   BOTTOM. *Hosta fortunei marginata alba*

with lustrous white flowers and a beautiful fragrance. The color range is not extensive, for all Hostas are white, pale lavender, blue-lilac or purple. This truly tough plant withstands considerable shade, may be left where it is, expanding the while, for twenty years with no complaint excepting a plea for water in times of extreme drought.

Where there is dappled sunshine and shadow or half time shade, day-lilies (Hemerocallis) offer us flowers from May to October. The botanical name implies that each flower is beautiful for a day, but there are many buds opening in succession on each of several stalks so we may be assured of weeks of bloom from each variety. There is no special time in which day-lilies must be planted, though they should be in the ground a month before frost. They are practically pest immune, care free, and any good garden soil (not rich) will satisfy them, but they will not bloom in deep shade.

We could start the day-lily season in May with the always popular lemon lily (Hemerocallis flava) with its clear yellow blossoms and graceful carriage, but this is only one of many species. In order to study the wide range of horticultural forms, the novice is wise to consult the catalogues of growers who specialize in day-lilies. We are told that there are many hundreds of named varieties in commerce today. It would be well to visit a nursery or public garden to see for ourselves these carefully labelled plants on display. As one becomes a true enthusiast one joins the flourishing Hemerocallis Society. The day-lily connoisseur selects critically, for he is interested in plant behavior even under such conditions as wind and rain; he cares about the manner in which the flowers fade (they should drop promptly but seldom do).

He notes how long a flower remains open and fresh; which varieties are effective at night; the carriage of foliage; the forms which excel as cut flowers; the fragrant ones and the miniatures.

The hybridizers are coming close now to a pure white day-lily, but apparently none yet are blue. Though the color of a day-lily in the wild is yellow or orange, here listed are some of the luscious hues of named varieties as they appear in the catalogues:

Pink: blush, coral, orchid, shrimp, flamingo, peach, pink melon
Red: cherry, ruby, oxblood, copper, raspberry, black-red, vermilion
Yellow: chartreuse, canary, gold, cadmium, maize, ivory, orange tones

Then there are wondrous bicolors and blends and those with lustrous sheen, with stripes and contrasting eye spots. And so may we paint garden pictures with undemanding day-lilies.

To introduce some stately perpendicular notes into our background plantings, the tall white spires of Cimicifuga should not be overlooked. These plants are known popularly as black cohosh, black snakeroot, bugbane—names with a forbidding connotation. By using several species we enjoy these casual plants from late June into October. They are true shade lovers, and, given a soil not too dry, they should thrive for many years with no care at all. The first to bloom is our own native C. racemosa whose flower spires rise from 4 to even 8 feet above the ground in July and August. Then the species davurica takes over to 5 feet high from August into fall. To carry on from there the species simplex, a mere 3 feet, blooms from September through much of October. When set against a dark background, Cimicifuga is striking both day and night.

If more summer and autumn color is desired, monkshood (Aconitum) or columbine (Aquilegia vulgaris) should give lasting satisfaction.

Thus do we plot and plan to garden easily in the shade. When once established this garden of little care should give us years of effortless pleasure.

Shaded Areas of a Sunny Herb Garden

There is fragrance and flavor and usefulness in a garden of herbs and there is much to know of history and legend associated with this ancient form of garden practice.

Sometimes herbs are arranged in beds to form a nicely designed geometric pattern. Or perhaps there is just a small plot for culinary herbs near the kitchen door, plants such as sun-loving chives, basil, parsley, dill or whatever one likes most. Often herbs are arranged simply in rows or set into groups in the flower border.

To plant and maintain a herb garden is comparatively simple, but most plants for such a garden require full sun. Watering is rarely necessary, and injurious insects seldom relish herb flavors. Flowers from a herb garden are on the whole not sensational, but the general character of plant growth, the silvery gray-green of much of the foliage lends a quiet charm and a special kind of interest, and to every visitor a nosegay of many scents. For indoors a big bouquet of freshly plucked branches and blossoms emits a faint aroma through the room from plants such as lavender, rose-mary, the mints, scented geraniums. The latter though not winter hardy in our climate is, in its many fascinating leaf forms, rarely omitted from a sunny herb garden.

Although the majority of herbs are happiest in full sun-shine, there is a small group which should prosper willingly in part time shade—that is in bright strong light; in inter-mittent sun and shadow; or in half shade.

Angelica (A. archangelica). Background plant to six feet tall with a tropical dramatic effect. Fragrant flowers in white umbels in June and July rise above the compound leaves. It prefers a fairly rich moist soil and grows easily from seed sown in the fall. This herb actually does not do well in full sun. If blossoms are removed before they fade, the plant will live and bloom the following year, but, being biennial, it will die after its second flowering. It will also self sow. Roots are commercially used in the making of certain liqueurs, herbal beverages and perfume. The stems make a kind of confection and the crushed seeds serve as flavoring.

Balm, Lemon Balm (Melissa officinalis). Much branched two foot tall perennial related to mint and somewhat weedy. The crenated leaves, heart-shaped at the base, are two inches long and of a bright green color. When crushed the foliage has an aromatic scent similar to that of lemon verbena and the taste resembles lemon peel. Inconspicuous flowers in late summer are cream color. It grows from seed or by division and should be transplanted when an inch tall. Lemon balm spreads rapidly and seems content almost anywhere in sun or half shade. Bees gather honey from the tiny blossoms.

Camomile (Anthemis nobilis). White daisy-like flowers on 12 inch stems. This fragrant perennial has wiry procumbent stems and feathery bright green foliage.

Catnip (Nepeta cataria). A perennial 2 to 3 feet tall with gray-green foliage, a spicy flavor and nondescript flowers. Of special interest to cats that will roll ecstatically in a sprig or nibble the leaves either fresh or dried.

Chervil (Anthriscus cerefolium). Resembles a delicate parsley plant with similar uses though its flavor is like a mild blend of anise and watercress. The blossoms are small, dainty and white. Very popular in French cookery, it being one of the "fines herbes" used in omelets or in salads. This aromatic annual grows $1\frac{1}{2}$ feet high in moderately rich soil. Sow where it is to remain and thin to stand no less than 6 inches apart. Midday summer sun causes chervil to wilt. It likes dappled sun and shadow or to be grown in a bright sunless spot in strong light.

Lemon-verbena (Lippia citriodora). A graceful plant to three feet high but not winter hardy north, though in its native habitat in hot countries it may grow into a ten foot shrub. The long narrow leaves have a lime or lemon flavor and fragrance. Sprigs are used to decorate summer drinks or fresh fruit desserts as one might use a wedge of lemon. Plants in pots are easily purchased.

Pineapple sage (Salvia rutilans). Much branched shrub to 4 feet, whose leaves have the aroma of pineapple. Bright red blossoms like tiny firecrackers appear in October. Not winter hardy north, but it makes a good house plant. Leaves are sometimes used to flavor fruit drinks.

Sweet cicely (Myrrhis odorata). Ornamental fern-like leaves with a flavor of licorice, and white flower umbels in summer. This perennial 2 to 3 feet tall is strongly attractive to bees. The shiny seeds nearly an inch long are filled with an anise-tasting oil. Sweet cicely may be propagated by division, or the seeds may be sown as soon as ripe, but will not germinate until spring.

Tansy (Tanacetum vulgare). Ornamental feathery foliage with a pleasant fragrance. Flowers are waxy yellow buttons in flat-top clusters in summer. Perennial to 3 feet, may be propagated by division of clumps.

Woad (Isatis tinctoria). Erect yellow panicles of effective bloom in late spring. A biennial, anciently used as a blue dye. Seeds planted in April will bloom the following year. Set plants 12-18 inches apart.

It is difficult to draw the line as to which plants actually belong in a herb garden, for of course most perennials are herbs in that they die to the ground when winter comes, though their roots survive. In the sense in which we here apply the term, a herb is an herbaceous plant used for seasoning, for flavor or garnish and for the production of perfume or in certain medicines. Some plants often included in a herb garden are treated in this book as general garden subjects. Among them are sweet woodruff (Asperula), bee-balm (Monarda), mint, wild ginger (Asarum), checkerberry (Gaultheria) and black snakeroot (Cimicifuga racemosa). And happily these are all shade plants.

To Edge a Walk or Border

IN ALMOST ANY DEGREE OF SHADE

To create a ribbon or flat-to-the-earth effect as edging for the flower bed or garden walk, bugle (Ajuga) is one of the best of plants. The close matted leaves seem appliqued to the soil, and the flower spikes, blue, purple, white or rose, range in height to from 4 to 14 inches according to the forms selected. They produce a cheerful band of color in spring. The kinds with metallic crinkled green leaves or those with bronze or silver tones create an unusual glint, of interest all season. Some forms spread rapidly from stolens, like the blue Ajuga reptans. Others are more static, as for instance its white form (Ajuga reptans alba) or the similar species Ajuga pyramidalis with its bright blue-violet blossoms.

Pachysandra and the ivies make good all year round bands. Ivies are charming also if trained to grow against a low support or wire edging to form a small hedge. Evergreen Christmas-fern is another deep shade tolerant plant which serves well as an edging, especially to a shrub border or a woodland walk.

Nothing could be easier to grow than white margined goutweed (Aegopodium podagraria variegatum) which is very shade tolerant and produces whitish flower umbels in June. Unless the form variegatum is used it were better not to consider this plant anywhere because the original gout-weed, plain Aegopodium podagraria, is an obnoxious weed. However, any roving plant reluctant to stay within bounds may be kept under control by the use of metal edging strips inserted vertically into the ground deep enough to deter the invading plant roots.

Pick-a-back-plants (Tolmiea menziesii), our western natives, are good edgers and, though winter hardy, they may be potted to serve as foliage plants indoors. The greenish flower sprays are not showy but the basal leaves are interesting and resemble those of foamflower (Tiarella cordfolia). Plantain-lilies (Hosta) are also basal-leaved. Some of these are suitable as edging plants especially the dwarf forms such as Hosta tardiflora and Hosta minor, both late bloomers.

IN HALF SHADE

Spreading out in a dense low cushion lambs-ears (Stachys lanata) serve as interesting edgers. They have furry silver-green leaves with purplish or pink flower stalks in June or July, which some gardeners cut away preferring the simplicity of the leaves alone. I remember a garden in which a planting of lambs-ears serves as a 2 foot wide edging to an identical pair of flower borders facing each other and separated by a greensward, the entire composition running at right angles to a terrace. At the far end there stands a piece of sculpture as focal point, backed by a planting of evergreens. A restful and memorable piece of landscape design.

Edging candytuft (Iberis sempervirens) has clouds of snowy white blossoms from late April to early June, and narrow evergreen foliage. Among the good varieties are 'Little Gem,' compact in growth, and the profusely flowering varieties 'Snowflake' or 'Purity.' In half shade bloom may be less prolific than if there were full sun. For neatness, the plants should be trimmed back after flowering.

Sweet woodruff (Asperula odorata) makes a dainty edging with its whorls of delicate slim leaves and masses of tiny white flowers in May and June. Another edging sometimes too casual for the formalized garden is dead-nettle (Lamium maculatum), with little silver-splashed leaves. The stems have a way of bending over at the base but the flower stalks are erect. The white-flowered form blends well with all other plants, blooming in June and July. Shear in midsummer to insure compact growth.

Epimedium in several species, so easy and tolerant, is content in even more than half shade. Its little waxen blossoms in yellow, crimson, lilac, white, appear in spring. The attractive leaves on short wiry stems sometimes remain into the winter. These low growing plants are spreading but not aggressively so.

Coral-bells (Heuchera species). Rosettes of basal leaves make a decorative edging. Many slender scapes of tiny gay blossoms in white, pink and fiery colors bloom from June through August.

Certain of the harebells or bellflowers should not be omitted as edging possibilities, especially Campanula carpatica and C. portenschlagiana, blooming white or blue in summer. The strong blue tone of flowering plumbago (Ceratostigma plumbaginoides) makes welcome bands of color as the season comes toward a close.

On a Paved Terrace in the Shade

STONES WITH SOME FLOWERING ACCOMPANIMENTS

I can think of no type of architecture to which a stone terrace might be inappropriate. Increasing interest seems to be shown in this type of landscape work which links together home and grounds. The house reaches into the garden through the medium of stone, and the garden creeps up into the stonework and settles down in beds and crevices especially arranged for its comfort.

Casement doors convey one from the house to a wide flagstone area, which is laid not too precisely, yet is not disturbingly irregular. To connect the terrace with gardens beyond, a group of steps has been provided, and thus one looks below to a restful lawn with trees and borders. The terrace faces northwest and includes a tall trunked tree which casts shade upon this out-of-door withdrawing-room. The tree is deciduous, so there is afternoon sun in winter and in early spring. Here is where one enjoys the sunset, and coffee after dinner. Even on a mild day in winter one wraps in a steamer rug, and on chaise-longue enjoys an hour's sunshine and the winter garden, which has been planned accordingly.

The project then is to clothe the shaded stone areas with evergreens and flowering perennials. The six details under consideration are as follows:

(1) Vines for the House Wall
(2) Plants for the Flagstone Crevices
(3) Plants in Pots
(4) Hedges for Terrace Edges
(5) Ring Around the Tree
(6) Retaining-Wall Garden

Vines for the House Wall. The garden on stone was planned before house construction had actually begun, so the sections to be planted were left unpaved. Most houses lend themselves to a green wall tracery, especially the brick and other masonry types. For the accommodation of vines, an oblong bed was provided at the intersection of house and terrace. This bed exists at points where vines are actually to be placed. Vine composition can bear a great deal more consideration than many think necessary. Setting plants in rows may produce an effect of sorts, but one vine strategically placed may, in time, create a picture of high artistic merit. I have heard of those who train their ivy into interesting patterns, like espaliered fruit trees.

The vine which comes first to mind is good old English ivy. Not necessarily the big-leaf form, but a very hardy form with smaller leaves—Hedera helix baltica. There are now many interesting forms of this species, and one variety, arborescens, makes a nice miniature bush. Ivy, as every one has probably discovered, is often stubborn about climbing. Young plants whose wood has not yet toughened are more energetic, but often they will not consent to climb at all unless they are in some way teased into it. (There are vine tacks and other clever supports for this purpose.) These vines like plenty of food for best development. Some one told us that ivies would grow like wild if we placed a wad of chopped beef under their roots. We were chuckling over this absurd contention, and lost no time in trying the experiment. Soon we found that all our ivies had been unearthed. The pup, whose nose was keener than ours, had traced that delicious putrefying meat, and he too made a "discovery," uprooted the plants and devoured the meatballs. For weeks thereafter he took extraordinary interest in all little plants, and, like Ferdinand, sniffed them fervently. But—he missed one plant, which grew so rapidly it was up the chimney in no time. (Don't try the experiment—fertilizer will make ivies grow just as well.)

More hardy than most ivies is Euonymus fortunei, with almond-shaped leathery leaves, and delectable small varieties, radicans or minimus. Variety vegetus, a climbing shrub, rewards us in time with handsome berries, orange and yellow, like bitter-sweet. The smaller varieties have no berries, but grow rapidly and cling closely by rootlike holdfasts.

Some gardeners shun Euonymus because of its susceptibility to scale insects. I would rather grow this interesting and useful plant and protect it by spraying with a miscible oil in spring before growth starts or keep close watch and treat it with the proper insecticide later if need be.

For rapid growth nothing exceeds the familiar Virginia creeper (one variety has smaller leaves), and the useful Boston ivy. They grow everywhere, their leaves turning red and yellow and bronze in autumn. These are all deciduous, but the very fine tracery pattern of woody stems against walls is not without interest, and the small berries on older plants are decidedly decorative.

Plants for the Flagstone Crevices. This terrace which is used as a living-room is furnished with chairs and tables. This fact had to be borne in mind when considering the flagstone crevices. Cementing was thought to be most practical, but, in out-of-the-way spots, tufted or rosetted rock plants were introduced. The earth pockets had been carefully filled with a mixture of sand, peat moss and loam, which is a good general formula. This mixture varied according to the requirements of the individual plants. Some minute plants were then introduced with restraint, for they could not interfere as one moved about the terrace. Friends should not be reminded to watch their step. Plants of creeping habit like Nepeta hederacea and Mentha requieni could run along the channels. Moss can be gathered up from places where it is not wanted, and laid in the furrows. The worse the drainage, the better it is likely to thrive, and it should be kept moist. Other little plants to grow between stones are Houstonia, Veronica, Ajuga, Arenaria, Mazus, and Sagina. These will move along the earth pockets and overflow upon the stone, and in their blooming season create fascinating pools of color. Sagina (pearlwort) if it once gets into the lawn may take possession of it, so beware. Most of these plants will not endure more than half shade.

Plants in Pots. There is a broad stone rail at the edge of this terrace. It is low and comfortable to sit upon. Plants in tubs make nice corner accents, or punctuate with color wherever needed. In small pot gardening one need not be too strictly bound to shade lovers, for if one longs for certain irresistibles which require extra sunlight, they may always be moved about into the sun for as long as necessary. Here we shall discuss only those plants which will stand half shade or more.

Among potted plants for formal effect, in large tubs, yew, box or privet clipped or not, are dignified almost anywhere and at all seasons, but box likes protection from too much winter sun. The familiar arbor-vitæ is shade-resistant, and its bright green color and crisp lacy texture make it a good garden subject (small forms preferred). Arbor-vitæ is apt to grow "leggy" if not clipped back early. As evergreen shrubs of compact habit and colorful bloom there are various azaleas like the hardy amœna, hinodegiri and some of the rhododendrons, especially those with small leaves and luscious bloom. The trouble with azalea amœna is not so

Dwarf pumila iris and forget-me-nots on a stone terrace

much its magenta bloom but that the flowers fade to a depressing brown. These may be removed, of course. The virtue of this plant is its hardiness, its evergreenness and the fine glossy foliage. Many new forms of azaleas are being introduced yearly. Leaves similar in effect may be had in the many forms of Japanese holly (Ilex crenata varieties) which are hardy and very useful. Most plants in tubs must have winter protection or be plunged into the ground before frost.

Many deciduous plants may be tried and taken away when their leaves die, such as hydrangeas. Begonias in their many forms add brilliance. In pot gardening plants should be chosen for their decorative composition, and tidy growth.

For a draping and picturesque effect, a gnarled old wisteria may be tried, and some clematis in lovely hybrid varieties with huge flowers. Fuchsias and lilies are very effective in pots as are the low growing and floriferous chrysanthemums. In a half-shaded place some interesting experiments might be tried with shaped wire upon which vines might festoon themselves. There is no end to the effects possible with long boxes and compositions of non-weedy material, and these may be whisked away at any time and replaced. (See Window Boxes on page 144.)

Hedges for Terrace Edges. Where there is no masonry edge to the terrace, a border of living shrubs is to be considered. A solid row of yews gives formal effect, and if the plants are a dwarf variety, their form is compact and the needles sturdy and deep green, and they may have a few succulent berries in autumn. The low bushy Euonymus (var. vegetus and carrierei) may be planted about a few feet apart, and for added grace might have some of their branches fastened down to the ground with strong hairpins. Ilex crenata (little leaf Japanese holly) in a choice of low growing forms resembling old box is extensively used as hedge material. English ivy in bush form makes an attractive low hedge. In half-shaded places daphne or candytuft looks beautiful. Both are evergreens and serve well as miniature hedges, or edgings. All the above materials are evergreen and all have flowers or fruits, excepting the small ivies.

Ring Around a Tree. Where it has been necessary in building the terrace to raise it above the soil level of existing trees, a solution to this problem can be met by surrounding the tree-well with a low wall. This makes the tree seem as though it were deep down in a huge flowerpot, on whose rim one might sit.

Retaining-Wall Garden. In viewing the terrace from a lower level one sees that it has been propped up by a retaining-wall built with well selected stones. Having been properly constructed, it has earth pockets which afford opportunities for the planting of a perpendicular garden. Some people like "blooming rocks," others prefer their planting to be more or less incidental, a sort of accompaniment to the stone. Leaf habit is here very important, for much of the success of this garden depends on the way in which the leaves behave between the stones and how they trail over them.

A few suggestions for the wall garden—plants which drape themselves over rocks or creep along the crevices:

Fumitory (Corydalis)

Ferns—polypody and spleenwort

Kenilworth ivy (Cymbalaria)

Auricula primrose

Bellflowers

(Campanula portenschlagiana, rotundifolia, and carpatica)

Most of the plants recommended for Flagstone Crevices would be appropriate here, see page 79.

White Flowers in the Shade

A white garden well composed is always in good taste (special emphasis on the word "composed"). Such a garden would be completely colorless unless it were set off with a good green background. If a white border is contemplated, plants should be selected whose foliage is handsome and long enduring. Lacking that, the plants may be interspersed with leathery-leaved ferns, low shrubs, or attractive ground covers to act as foils.

A rock garden planted exclusively with white flowers might have its charm, if, for weight and balance, the value of leaf and rock were given careful consideration in the composition. The effect otherwise might be somewhat ghostly.

There are many small perennials to be considered—too many to list here, excepting these few in passing. The white variety of Lamium is a pleasant little edging plant which grows almost anywhere and has a long blooming season.

The small leaves are splashed with white, and the plant does well in half or even more shade. White baneberry has effective flowers, good foliage, and china-white berries, each with a black "pupil" like a doll's eye. Barrenwort (Epimedium), another good subject, has attractive foliage and does well under trees.

A garden predominantly green, or where green and white share the honors, may be a thing of vast beauty. There is more variation in white than one might realize, and the off-white is not to be scorned. Think of the cream white of Astilbe, and the various casts of lavender in anemones. There is a suggestion of green in the feathery bloom of virgins-bower and purity in the white of a plantain-lily. Should the tone of milky bellflower be white or cream? To me it has a bluish cast. All these subtle variations in shade enhance the interest in a green and white garden.

The Garden at Night

With the coming of dusk, color in the landscape vanishes. The blues and purples and reds which delight us in daytime are blotted out when night comes. Only the white and palest pastel flowers are visible, especially when they glisten in the moonlight. Many gardeners can, and do, resort to simulated moonlight by installing electric spotlights and using white or blue bulbs. This is a challenging study in itself, not to emulate the effect of a daytime garden but to give the illusion that the moon has created the picture, and requires subtle handling. Where artificial lighting is introduced, plants with colored blossoms may come into the picture, but to display our plant arrangements in blatant night lighting might be in questionable taste.

Imagine some of the possibilities in natural night light. Early spring is too cold a time to linger in the garden after dark, but we do want to observe all the small harbingers of the season from indoors at close range. So we have deliberately planned a garden composition accordingly. Perhaps there is a narrow brick-enclosed ledge at the foot of a great window, and beyond, a feeding station where in daytime we watch the winter birds at close view from the window. Here we wait to see the early bulbs emerge from the snow.

So we draw aside the window curtains and see, even in winter, in a sheltered corner the Christmas-rose (Helleborus) thrusting up its white, purple-flushed blossoms through the snow. The rows of buds on the Japanese andromeda are waiting to open their white bells later. At their feet winter aconite, like yellow buttercups, glow faintly while the snow lingers. Then there are little groups of snow-drops, snowflakes and chionodoxa in close succession together with hepaticas, primroses and spring beauties (Claytonia) all in white bloom. And winter honeysuckle displays its fragrant white blossoms.

A little later the white stars of bloodroot delight us as they emerge from their leafy overcoats. As companions there are white violet, early anemones, Siberian squills and the small species tulips in white with carmine trimmings. White grape hyacinths flower near by. The waiting buds on the andromeda have now burst into parchment bloom. Across the lawn, by some evergreens, the wraithlike shad-bushes are in clouds of white bloom, their silvery leaves

emerging. So may we from indoors enjoy the night garden in the early days of spring.

In May the fringe of woodland sparkles with great white trilliums and arching solomons-seal. A drift of white narcissus increases with the years. Backed by hemlocks, white azaleas and rhododendrons are coming into bloom, and masses of Spanish squills intermingle with ascending fern heads. Fragrant mock-orange is in bud and a graceful silverbell tree makes pleasant tracery. A Chinese wisteria stands alone, trained as a tree. It blooms like a white fountain above its twining stems and silvery-gray bark.

Now summer approaches and we enjoy the terrace at night, we sit by the pool, or we picnic in the play area. Near by some scented plantings have been arranged. There will be fragrant hesperis which has become naturalized under the trees. Tall accents are to be seen in white filipendula and sweet pepperbush. Summer phlox mingles with regal lilies, and flowering tobacco blooms all summer.

As the months progress into July and August there is more dramatic white bloom from large-flowered clematis as it climbs upon its pillar, and silver lace vine is festooned over a trellis. Tall snakeroot (Cimicifuga racemosa) is joined by showy Japanese lilies (Lilium speciosum), and later, Chinese white lilies (L. leucanthum var. chloraster) are intermingled with another snakeroot, the Kamtschatka species. There are floribunda roses where the daytime shade is only partial, and a tumbled edging of woolly lambs-ears (Stachys lanata) which shimmer silver in the night light. Fireflies electrify the air and the slender-winged hawkmoth seeks nectar in the blossoms.

WHITE FLOWERING PLANTS

A Selection

Shrubs

Amelanchier (shadbush)

Azalea, species and forms

Clematis
  (large flowered hybrids)

Clematis paniculata
  (sweet autumn C.)

Cornus florida
  (flowering dogwood)

Clethra (sweet pepperbush)

Halesia (silverbell tree)

Kalmia (mountain-laurel)

Philadelphus (mock-orange)

Leucothoë

Lonicera fragrantissima (fragrant
  winter honeysuckle)

Magnolia virginiana
  (sweetbay M.)

Pieris Japonica
  (Japanese andromeda)

Polygonum aubertii
  (silver lace vine)

Rhododendron, species and forms

Roses (trailing, climbing, shrubs)

Wisteria (Chinese white variety)

Perennials

Ajuga (white bugle)

Anemone canadensis (meadow A.)

Anemone japonica (Japanese A.)

Aruncus (goat's beard)

Astilbe

Cimicifuga racemosa and C. simplex (snakeroot)

Chrysanthemum arcticum

Filipendula

Hesperis (dames-rocket)

Lilium leucanthum var. chloraster [centifolium]
  (Chinese white L.)

Lilium regale (regal L.)

Lilium speciosum
  (showy Japanese L.)

Phlox paniculata
  (summer perennial P.)

Hosta plantaginea
  (fragrant plantain-lily)

Trillium grandiflorum
  (large flowering T.)

Sanguinaria (bloodroot)

Stachys (lambs-ears)

Vinca
  (white periwinkle)

Others

Seasonal bulbs	Impatiens (patience plant)
Begonia	Vinca rosea
(tuberous rooted, others)	(Madagascar periwinkle)

Annuals: Nicotiana alata grandiflora (jasmine tobacco)

Birds and Berries in the Shade

To those who seek ways and means of luring song birds into the garden, the following planting suggestions are offered.

It is a pity we cannot have our berries and let the birds eat them too! Yet, my neighbor's gardener tells me that he eats all the strawberries which the birds have pecked, and so, as he says, "we all have our fill."

All the birds do not like all berries. They have their preferences, and sometimes shun the prettiest berries, though they later eat them reluctantly, as a last resort. They are sometimes so distracted by feasting upon certain berries that they overlook all other fruits. They love elderberries, for instance, and will leave the raspberries and blackberries for you, if you hurry. Many birds turn up their beaks at apples and pears if there's a good thornapple in sight.

Have you noticed that most birds do not touch the berries on flowering dogwood until almost winter? Why? Because the fruit is bitter until after the first frost. How they love the dogwood family and its berries! Yet some birds do not particularly relish these fruits, for example, the meadowlark, oriole, scarlet tanager, wren and probably others.

Nevertheless, these berries must be popular, for more than eighty species of birds consider them excellent fare. The shadbush and spicebush are great favorites and so are Virginia creeper and wild grape. Many birds like to nest in the privet and others to hide in the hemlocks.

SOME SHADE PLANTS INTERESTING TO BIRDS

(For food, nesting, shelter)*

Trees

Amelanchier canadensis
   (shadbush)
Cornus florida
   (flowering dogwood)

Crataegus crus-galli
   (cockspur thorn) and others
Prunus virginiana (choke-cherry)
Thuja (American arbor-vitæ)

Tsuga (hemlock)

Shrubs

Aronia (chokeberry)
Lindera (spice-bush)
Cornus, many species
Diervilla lonicera
   (dwarf bush-honeysuckle)
Ilex crenata (Japanese holly)
Ilex glabra (inkberry)
Ilex verticillata
   (winterberry, black alder)
Leycesteria
   (Formosa honeysuckle)
Ligustrum (Privet)

Lonicera morrowi, and tatarica
   (honeysuckle)
Rhamnus frangula
   (alder buckthorn)
Wild roses (especially Rosa rugosa
   and R. humilis)
Symphoricarpos (snowberry)
Symplocus (Asiatic sweetleaf)
Taxus canadensis (American yew
   and other yews)
Vaccinium species (blueberry)
Viburnum (practically all species)

*I have been greatly aided in the compilation of this list by a pamphlet published by the National Audubon Society, Song-Bird Sanctuaries, by Roger T. Peterson

Vines

Celastrus scandens
(bitter-sweet)

Parthenocissus quinquefolia
(Virginia creeper)

Parthenocissus tricuspidata
(Boston ivy)

Ground Covers

Arctostaphylos (bearberry)

Cornus canadensis
(bunchberry)

Gaultheria (wintergreen)

Mitchella (partridge-berry)

Flowers Attractive to Humming Birds

Aquilegia (columbine)

Azalea

Campanula (bellflower)

Fuchsia

Hemerocallis (day-lily)

Heuchera (coral bells)

Lilium (lilies)

Lobelia (cardinal flower)

Lonicera (honeysuckle)

Monarda (beebalm)

Nicotiana
(flowering tobacco)

Physostegia (false dragonhead)

Weigela

Autumn and Winter Color

When the growing season has come to an end, and the last flower petals have fluttered to earth, our attention focuses upon the evergreens, the color of autumn foliage, twigs, seed pods, and berries. The provident gardener seeks ways and means of prolonging interest in the out-of-doors through the appropriate choice of shrubs which will brighten the winter landscape.

Visualize with me, if you will, a border which has been arranged for the special purpose of creating color when the flowering season is spent. This planting flanks the margin of a shaded path sufficiently wide to afford light and air in the growing season. It is here where we take our daily walks and enjoy the autumn picture. Later we swish through the carpet of fallen leaves grown crisp and sere, and we listen, as they crackle, when we trample them down. Then the snow comes, and sleet storms glaze the branches and bend them low.

THE AUTUMN SCENE

Against the lacy pattern of gray-green hemlocks are the touselled yellow flowers of the witch-hazel, upon whose naked stems the orange-berried bitter-sweet festoons itself. At its feet stands the bronze-leafed Pieris. The rich green yews are flecked with carmine berries, while the cones of arbor-vitæ are brown, the color of earth.

The burning-bush is ablaze with vermilion fruits the color of flame. There are cockspur thorns with little red apples, and a great pack of dogwoods whose berries are red, white, and blue. The jewel-like tones of the sassafras—emerald, mottled, tourmaline, amber, are in harmony with viburnums, enkianthus and virginia creeper, the color of whose leaves, as the sun shines through, is like all the wines of Burgundy.

THE WINTER SCENE

When the leaves have fallen and winter comes there is much to enjoy, and the scene still lures us. There are white birches near whose forked trunks lies a carpet of reddish-leaved Euonymus fortunei coloratus. Groups against dark evergreens to display their garlands of berry-beads—black, blue, white, and vermilion—are such shrubs as red chokeberry, snowberry, viburnum and bitter-sweet, berry feasts for birds.

As a study in leaf tone and texture we have the yellow, blue, and silver-greens in needle-leaf and lace-leaf evergreens. Then we see yellow, red, and bronze-green in the leaves of mahonia and leucothoë. The tones of box and pachistima and mountain laurel varied in texture and form, yet blend in lovely harmony.

With a background of snow that versatile dogwood tribe delights us still with its garnet, gold and coral twigs, and the kerria with jade. But nature allows no anticlimax here, for haven't we purple flowers from February daphne, and fragrant white from winter honeysuckle, and more witch-hazels in apricot and gold, blooming before April is launched? There are snowdrops, snowflakes, crocus, and winter aconite—and spring is near.

RÉSUMÉ OF PLANT MATERIAL SUGGESTED IN THE PRECEDING SECTION, AUTUMN AND WINTER COLOR

Evergreen

Buxus (box)	Pachistima
Euonymus (E. fortunei coloratus)	Pieris
Kalmia (mountain-laurel)	Taxus (yew)
Leucothoë	Thuja (arbor-vitæ)
Mahonia	Tsuga (hemlock)

Snowdrops (*Galanthus*) which cannot wait for spring

Bulbs

Crocus

Eranthis (winter-aconite)

Galanthus (snowdrop)

Leucojum (snowflake)

Deciduous

Aronia arbutifolia
  (red chokeberry)

Celastrus scandens (bitter-sweet)

Cornus (dogwood)

Crataegus crus-galli
  (cockspur thorn)

Daphne mezereum

Enkianthus

Euonymus atropurpureus
  (burning-bush)

Hamamelis (autumn and winter
  witch-hazels)

Kerria

Lonicera fragrantissima
  (winter honeysuckle)

Parthenocissus
  (Virginia creeper)

Sassafras

Symphoricarpos (snowberry)

Viburnum species

Enjoyment of the Garden

A visitor stood with me on the terrace of our home one summer's day. As we looked down upon the evergreen garden at the lower reaches of which is a long woodland pool, she said:

"How you must enjoy those garden chairs there at the water's edge. How pleasant it must be to sit quietly and contemplate this restful scene." "But I never have time for that," I replied, "the hour for meditation never comes." And then we both laughed.

How seldom do we actually give ourselves completely to the pleasures of the garden! We enjoy working and planning for it, and that of course is as it should be. But do we sometimes allow ourselves the luxury of complete and relaxed abandon to its beauties?

Some day soon let us try a cure for tension. We shall stroll into the garden promising ourselves to criticize nothing at all. We shall give not a thought to insect or spray, weeds or the garden hose. We shall carry neither trowel nor clippers. We may, if we choose, take a cushion and a book and (what is part of the game) a relaxed and cheerful mind. This is the time for complete enjoyment and nothing else. We are bent upon giving pleasure to our seeing, hearing, feeling, smelling and tasting. The five senses are going on a spree.

Our eyes are going to see beauty only, and design in deep shadow patterns across the green lawn. We shall look beyond the trees to blue skies where we trace the billowy cloud forms. In the shaded border we note the beauty of young buds unfolding and the color vibrations in flowers. We move into hot sunlight and return to cool shade where the tones change to minor keys—gold, indigo, mulberry and all the tertiary shades. We note the hues of primroses down the shaded path and compare the velvety tones of petals. Nature will, if only we realize it, help us in planning our color schemes. Her ideas in the color harmony of one flower alone may give us a clue to that unsolved problem in decoration. We shall observe the tones of earth and tree trunk and the lovely color variations in rock.

RIGHT. Primrose-bordered path with narcissus, ferns and forget-me-not

We shall stroll down to the pool in the shade and rest upon a garden bench. We look down into the depths of the quiet water and realize that we had never before noticed such reflections. But why? we ask ourselves. Why do we see so much this day? The greater our peace, the greater our vision.

A chipmunk will sit on his haunches and blink at us from the great rock over there, and we forget to wonder if it was he who ate last year's lily bulbs. (Or was it a mouse?—a rabbit?) A faint breeze will stir and if we listen we shall hear the murmur of pines. We wander down towards the bird sanctuary and hear the twitter and splash of young birds bathing. We shall feel the furry texture of fern fronds, and follow with our fingers those curled-up croziers. We shall touch the smooth white bark of birches, and then we'll sit upon a mossy bank and stroke that soft green cushion. The wild azalea must be in bloom, for we smell its delicate perfume. Can one remember the aroma of flowers? Is it possible mentally to anticipate the fragrance of lilacs—orchids—lilies—grapes?

We retrace our steps, and, homeward bound, pause to gather some fragrant mint at the water side. How good it tastes! But soon we shall the more enjoy its aroma in a frosty julep cup.

How relaxed we'll be, with all our senses soothed and satisfied. And tomorrow? Well, that is another day.

✣ 5 ✣

GARDEN DETAILS

Paths with a Purpose

A garden path is a means to an end, and more, if its margins, through appropriate planting, hold our interest. In the following section three types of paths are discussed—the trail—the wider path—the lane.

WILD WOODLAND TRAIL

The simplest of all paths is a trail, usually a rough-hewn single-file blaze through the woods. It should lead to somewhere, be it a brook, a pool, or a quiet glade where great families of ferns and their associates are assembled. It may lead to a hilltop view, or down to a sheltered retreat where fragile exotics are gathered together. A path of this character will require no surfacing whatever. Tanbark is pleasant under foot but it washes easily and rolls away. Nothing should disturb the naturalness nor mar the woodland picture. Care must be taken that surface roots and stumps be removed, for these might easily cause trouble. It is pleasant to find on such a trail as this an occasional resting-place. For this purpose a beautiful flat rock, or a smooth tree stump entwined with close-creeping vines, would be welcome. A huge log looks well among low ferns. A simple bench is in

good taste, provided it be not too sleek or too worldly in spirit.

FORMALIZED WOODLAND PATH

Here is where wild nature has been somewhat tamed. In this type of garden, natural vegetation has been thinned out, and careful grooming and more studied compositions have been introduced. A wider path is here appropriate. The shade is less deep, and a more sophisticated atmosphere prevails. There are Japanese yews and varieties of holly and hybrid rhododendrons. Drifts of flowering bulbs and primroses, natives and foreigners, are carelessly yet carefully composed, for here the shade is high and open. For a firm surface a path of this character may have a few inches of soil removed, and replaced with ashes. Some of the soil may be raked back into the top surface to tone down the alien gray color, and the whole then sprinkled and rolled. A mixture of coarse sand and fine gravel could be substituted for the ashes. This would leave a firm surface, pleasant to walk upon. There is also to be had a top dressing, which, if its gray color be not offensive, is very desirable. It is composed of very fine slate chips, in pieces not much bigger than the shavings from a fat pencil.

There are advantages to this wider-than-a-trail path. Two strollers may walk side by side and conversation is easier. Sufficient space is thus allowed that one need neither brush against a fragile flower nor ruin his clothes upon a moisture-laden branch or a prickly shrub. In stretches along this path where moisture might collect, stepping stones are snugly embedded. They should not be so far apart that the short-legged must leap from one stone to the next. In cases where the ground is very low and moist, under-drainage may be necessary. Probably a log bridge would suffice. This might be fashioned of two parallel logs across which are nailed close together sapling logs or even split ones with interesting bark.

A GARDEN LANE

Why should one not create deliberately a situation whereby a greater variety of plant material may be given an opportunity to grow, and yet retain a walk which is shaded?

Let us then make a fringe by cutting a broad path right through the thicket. This lane will be wide, almost like a narrow wagon road. Our choice of plant material is thus greatly augmented, and we may now be assured of shade for half the time, and the pleasant opportunity of planting the borders appropriately.

What could be more agreeable under foot than a broad green strip of grass carpeting this path? It would seem as though the lawn were flowing into the new opening-up of the woods. Such a cut as this should be at least twenty feet wide—perhaps six feet on each side for shrubs and flowers, and the center for easy strolling. Imagine the delicate beauty of gray birches, of tall ferns, and astilbe plumes in half-shade.

This path would probably be winding, and yet it might quite well be straight, serving not only as an interesting promenade, flanked by broken borders, but as a vista to some focal point beyond. At the end of this avenue there may be a rich planting of evergreens as background for garden sculpture and a pool. The possibilities are far-flung and tempting. This greensward could be flanked by a border loosely hedged with holly and hemlock, and a festoon of climbing roses in the margin, for these will be happy in half shade.

Consider here an arrangement of deciduous shrubs, old favorites, planned for succession of bloom:

Forsythia	Azalea
Weigela	Summer sweet (Clethra)
Honeysuckle	Hydrangea
Mock-orange	Japanese quince
Rose acacia	Sweet shrub (Calycanthus)

With a careful eye to grouping this could make a charming picture. One should be mindful of the woodland to right and left, drawing attention to it by every means possible, and not shutting it off by rigid screenlike planting. Narrow paths may swerve off into the woods at intervals to create a melding of wild and formalized arrangements, all flowing into one another by means of paths.

Steps

A few styles in steps are here discussed, but only those which lend themselves to the accompaniment of incidental planting. Almost all the plant material has been selected so that at all seasons of the year something near the steps will be in leaf, in flower, or in berry.

FIVE STEP ARRANGEMENTS

We have been conducted through the beautiful grounds of a vast estate. We have strolled from terrace to lawn, from sunken garden down to a formalized woodland, and we now rest upon a great, smoothly polished log, laid horizontal, at the lower reaches of a wild woodland dell. We have descended a great many steps at intervals during this pilgrimage, and yet we were not conscious of them. Why? They fitted their environment, they were firmly built and comfortable to step upon. Now, as we retrace our way over the wooded hillside, we shall make notes of the structure and planting of the various types of treads and risers.

Starting then with the steps in the wild part of the garden, we find that the first short group is fashioned of slabs of weathered oak, the rough bark side comprising the riser. There is growing here a colony of tiny polypody-ferns, and at the step ends Christmas-ferns and round-leaved violets, which have yellow flowers, the leaves later forming a handsome ground cover.

We follow along the path amid interesting woodland flora until we come to the next ascent—steps in groups of three. A slim white birch log is propped against the riser, and the broad tread is carpeted in emerald-green moss. Near by are acid-loving plants like shortia, wintergreen, galax, and partridge-berry, and in the moss is a tiny evergreen trailer, which in its season has china-white berries—creeping snowberry.

From this point we wind our way into a lighter shade, and gradually come upon a more formalized woodland. Here we

climb a short flight of low-curving steps made with large flat-top stones embedded carefully and firmly into the earth. Here there are light shade and stippled sunshine through near-by trees. In mossy risers are patches of ferns, and a bouquet of dead-nettle (Lamium), whose flowers are like little snapdragons. In the rock work arranged casually at the step ends are pachistima with its dainty evergreen leaves, and rattlesnake-fern with "fruits" in late summer. Delicate epimedium blooms here in spring and spreads its effective leaves gracefully.

We have now emerged into the open and stand upon a great expanse of shadowy lawn with contours rising toward the house. Here, embedded in the sod, near some shimmering poplars, which shade us from the sun, is a step of silvery-gray wood four inches square at the ends. This forms the riser and the front of the tread, the remainder of the tread being grass. There are several of these steps a few feet apart. A small hole has been bored in the wood (or was it an accommodating knot hole?) In this crevice is growing, in a few thimblefuls of earth, Sedum acre. The ends of the steps are planted with a tumbled mass of Daphne cneorum, lovely all the year, but only so if in a spot to its liking and no more than half shade.

Finally we reach the garden steps which lead us once more to the house terrace. Here there is shade for half the day. The risers are thin horizontal layers of shale-like stone, and the treads are of heavy flagging. If any cement has been used it is not visible on the surface. Here and there in earth pockets among chinks are growing ever-blooming Kenilworth ivy, fumitory (Corydalis) and polypody ferns.

Water in the Shaded Garden

THE ARTIFICIAL POOL WITH SUGGESTED PLANTINGS

The stylized pool, or one which follows a frankly geometric form, be it a circle, an oval, an oblong or even a segment, may have its borders planted, or it may, in perfectly good taste, remain quite unadorned. But the pool which attempts to simulate nature will have its borders treated with utmost care, and this is not at all an easy matter. The gardener will certainly wish to avoid a monotonous fringe of unrelated plants. Skillful rockwork without visible cement is one of the best settings for plant material.

THE REFLECTION POOL

This can be made a very decorative feature in the design of an open garden of many trees. This great mirror will be placed with care so that nothing uninteresting may come within the ranges of its reflection. A dignified frame for such a mirror in the shade is a closely clipped wreath of dwarf yew to mask completely the pool's edge—and nothing else, no aquatic, nothing to interfere with the carefully planned picture. (The clouds will form their own pattern.) Instead of the dwarf yew, a ring of roses will do well in half shade; Rose wichuriana would be perfect around this pool. It is easily pegged down, has handsome glossy leaves, and after blooming can be kept in trim by severe pruning. (To avoid black spot, be careful not to plant roses too near the water.)

POOL IN LIGHT TO FULL SHADE

This pool is built in the shade of evergreen trees. It has a massing of tall shrubs as a background, and low ones in the foreground and about its rim. The material chosen all comes under the heading of heaths or Ericaceæ, whose requirement is acid soil. Every plant here is native of our American woodland, and all of it is evergreen. The plants are not only ornamental as woodland subjects, but are among the choicest evergreens for the most formal gardens.

The tallest plant among them, placed at the rear, is Rhododendron maximum, in front of which is mountain-laurel. Then comes Pieris floribunda. Draped about the pool at the rear is Leucothoë. Small plants among rocks are trailing arbutus, wintergreen (Gaultheria), box huckleberry (Gaylussacia), and creeping snowberry (Chiogenes). Two other charming small plants are shinleaf (Pyrola) and pipsissewa (Chimaphila). Every plant in this association has attractive flowers, berries, or capsules. Remember that all these plants demand an acid soil excepting Pieris and Leucothoë, though they too prefer it.

POOL IN VARYING DEGREES OF SHADE, FEATURING AZALEAS AND BULBS

Here is a formalized garden with a well-groomed planting around a pool. It is set in the very lowest spot in a light and airy wooded tract, and the shade is high with intermittent sunlight. Steps lead down to this dell or bowl, and the sides are steep banks completely clothed in all sorts of rhododendrons. These are chosen for succession of bloom, and, though most of them are evergreen, some of the azaleas are deciduous. The glossy leaves glisten in the sun splotches, and from April into July there are white and pink and lavender blooms, but the salmon, yellow, and heavy tones are carefully placed to avoid a clashing of color.

The pool is surrounded by a casual path with broad flagged areas for garden chairs. The rock work at the pool edge affords opportunities for choice shrubs and for incidental herbaceous plants.

At about the time when the dogwoods are in bloom and mountain-laurel is beginning to be, chrome-yellow azaleas are mirrored in the water. Japanese yew spreads over the edge, its broadest arm toward the water, and a massing of hairbells (Campanula) cascades in half shade.

Among the rocks we have seen throughout the spring a pageant of flowering bulbs. In the brightest spots there were crocuses with bugle (Ajuga) to cover their leaves while they ripen. There were snowdrops and snowflakes. Trout-lilies were there, or perhaps you still prefer to call them dog-tooth violets, though they are not violets, but belong to the lily family. These bloom in many colors, and they even drift up among the shrubs on the bank side, or nestle against a tree trunk. Periwinkle or sweet woodruff is planted above them, because their leaves soon disappear. The obliging little scilla tribe was there, happy in almost any shade.

Down the shaded path as far as one can see narcissus and daffodils have become naturalized and bloom in May and June. At this season blue flag iris appears with its sword-like leaves. Lilies then carry on the procession, and are planted in such a way that their unsightly dying stalks may be hidden.

To Grow Among Small Bulbs

Ajuga (bugle)   Asperula (sweet woodruff)

Lysimachia (moneywort)   Myosotis (forget-me-not)

Oxalis (wood-sorrel)   Trientalis (starflower)

Maidenhair-fern, others

Companions for Tall Bulbs Such as Lilies

Thalictrum (meadow-rue) vari-   Ferns, such as the interrupted-
ous species   fern and goldie-fern

Hosta
(plantain-lily)

Summer and Autumn Bloom in Fairly Dry Soil

In spring our garden soils generally contain a fair amount of moisture, but as the season advances, some areas dry out to a considerable degree. The plants discussed here are not moisture demanding; however, where the soil is mostly sand or is thin and powdery it will require some humus, compost or other moisture retaining material to give the plant roots a firm foundation.

Aster cordifolius (blue wood aster). In September and October arching sprays of small violet flowers on a plant 4 to 5 feet tall. Content in half shade and almost any soil. Best in wild garden. The white wood aster (A. divaricatus), less tall, blooms at about the same time but is too rough for the cultivated garden, though it stands much shade. Fringe of woodland or wild garden.

Campanula carpatica (Carpathian harebell or bellflower). A low growing little plant usually less than a foot tall, for rock garden, in a wall or as a border edging. Bright blue or white saucer-shaped flowers July and August in half shade. Blooming at about the same time is the

Dalmatian bellflower or wall harebell (Campanula portenschlagiana) with star-like blue-purple flowers and foliage to form a close mat. Identical to the bluebells of Scotland is Campanula rotundifolia. It blooms also in July and August, and likes a wall crevice from which it may cascade down.

Ceratostigma plumbaginoides (plumbago). A fine border and edging plant to 1 foot high with intense gentian blue flowers in August and September. Half shade. It starts growth late.

Corydalis lutea. Fern-like leaves on this dainty plant with pale yellow blossoms for most of the summer. Useful in wall or rock garden, for joints of steps, stony banks, borders. To 8 inches tall. It self sows. Half shade.

Dicentra eximia (wild or fringed bleeding-heart). A familiar and easy-going plant with its lacy leaves and dusty-rose blossoms all summer. It grows to 18 inches tall. Rock garden, border or woodland. Will bear considerable shade.

Digitalis ambigua (yellow foxglove). To 3 feet tall, blooming in June and July. Flowering at about the same time is the common foxglove (D. purpurea), slightly taller with purple, rose white or pink blossoms. Light to half shade.

Eupatorium rugosum (white snakeroot). Not to be confused with black snakeroot (Cimicifuga). A bushy plant to 4 feet tall, having masses of small white flowers in August and September. Most effective in a wild garden, it stands fairly deep shade.

Filipendula hexapetala (dropwort, meadowsweet). A plant under three feet tall with lacy foliage and tiny fragrant white blossoms in June. Border or wild garden in half shade. There are several other species of various heights.

Hesperis matronalis (dames-rocket). Though preferring moisture this plant is easily satisfied. It resembles tall phlox with purple, lilac or white blossoms in June and July. Fringe of woodland or rear border in half to light shade.

Lamium maculatum (dead nettle). Flowers from May to July resemble small purplish or white snap-dragons. A plant to 1 ½ feet with small

silver blotched leaves. Casual or carefree in a wild garden, among rocks or informal edging, but a rapid spreader blooming in May to July.

Lilium (lilies). Several species are recommended such as the orange-scarlet Carolina lily, the apricot nankeen lily, orange tiger lily and the predominantly white regal lily. Most of these bloom in July. Half shade.

Malva moschata (musk mallow). A showy plant to 2 feet high with rose or white single fragrant blossoms to 2 inches across. A good plant for the border, flowering almost all summer in half shade.

Monarda didyma (bee-balm). This and the species M. fistulosa (wild bergamot) are bushy plants 3 to 4 feet high. Blossoms are scarlet or shades of pink, white, lilac or purple from June to August. For border woodland or herb garden in light to half shade.

Oenothera fruticosa (evening-primrose) and its varieties are 1 to 3 feet tall with showy sulphur yellow flowers two inches across in June and July. Effective in the border in half shade.

Saponaria officinalis (bouncing bet). The name applies to its rapid spreading. To 3 feet with pink or white flowers from June to August in light to half shade.

Veronica officinalis (common speedwell). Trailing plant with flower racemes of pale blue from May to July. Good ground cover, rough and spreading, useful under trees. Light to full shade.

Ground Covers

There is of course nothing that can take the place of grass where a large carpet of green is wanted. It stands a great deal of punishment, for we may walk upon it, play

LEFT. Vari-colored foxgloves blend well with sulphur evening-primroses (*Oenothera fruticosa*).

upon it, within reason, and no other ground cover is as inexpensive to sow nor as rapid to mature, though the question of maintenance is ever to be dealt with. Perhaps some day grass growth may be harmlessly retarded, for scientists are at work developing sprays to this end. However, mechanized mowing does lessen labor, yet edging is wearisome, though this chore may be eased by the use of edging plants, by stonework or again by labor-saving machinery.

Ground cover planting materials will always be needed for many situations. We need them where grass refuses to grow under trees. Ground covers serve a decorative purpose near steps, by stone walls, among rocks, by fences and banks where grass mowing might be difficult. Some lovely effects may be had with ground covers which display sheets of color in their season.

For success, and a minimum of care in growing ground covers, let us select plant materials which are suited by their nature to the areas in which we wish them to grow. If we live in an area where the ecological associates are evergreen trees and oaks there should be good rich acid soil and there we shall plant ground covers which revel in this locality. We can actually create the proper soil but this entails continuous and careful effort. Fortunately most ground covers are content in ordinary, more or less neutral soil.

Low growing and spreading shrubs make excellent ground covers. They are more costly than perennials but they cover a large space at the start. If bare areas are left between them we have to think about weeding or perennial ground covers to fill in. Yet buckwheat hulls, ground cocoa shells or similar materials when spread between shrubs discourage weeds and give a neat brown look, and these eventually turn into humus. I usually spread hulls from one to two inches deep, and they lend a trim look to the borders. In much frequented places near the house one would probably consider shrubs which are evergreen, for these would be attractive the whole year around.

Certain ground-hugging perennials may be stepped upon, but most of them resent this, and some of the succulent sedums crush messily underfoot. If we wish deliberately to bar trespassing, some of the woody vines make a good rough ground cover barrier, and they fill the space rapidly. They may be pegged down, but if they come in contact with any other plants they will start climbing both horizontally and vertically.

How high can a plant grow and still be classed as a ground cover? Let us say under two feet and a half for shrubs, but much lower for perennials. Some ground cover plants are often sold in large tufts or mats. These can be separated into little segments and planted some distance apart. Thus do we economize. And we try to determine approximately how long the gaps will remain unfilled and how much weeding we must do in the meanwhile. Therefore we should try to find out if the plants selected are quick growing or slow. The soil should be prepared with great care and with generous thought to plant expansion.

As for bank coverage, large healthy plants should be chosen whether they are vines or shrubs. Plants which die to the ground in winter are usually not advisable for banks because heavy rains and melting snow can cause erosion and heave out those little plants which have slight anchorage.

Let us remember that the more the plants are content in their environment the less maintenance is necessary. It is therefore good gardening to give the plants soil and situation to their liking. Before the plants become well established it is usually necessary to fertilize and to mulch. One way to accomplish the former is to cast a mixture of powdered fertilizer and sand and then water them down if the plants are very close together. We mulch with well-rotted manure, humus, compost, peat moss or other organic matter. The acid-demanding plants will appreciate scrapings from the woodland floor where the soil has an acid reaction.

A SELECTION OF GROUND COVERS FOR VARIOUS SITUATIONS

(See Part II for Plant Characteristics and Shade Requirements)

FOUNDATION PLANTING WITH LOW GROWING EVERGREENS AS GROUND COVERS

Much of our contemporary domestic architecture, with its low lines and large expanse of glass, calls for planting materials which complement the scale of the house and do not obstruct a view from the windows. For their year around beauty most gardeners prefer a predominance of evergreens, and wide bands of ground covers.

Japanese holly (Ilex crenata). Where dwarf box might not be sufficiently hardy or too slow in growing, the low forms of Ilex crenata are much used. According to *Hortus*, variety helleri should grow no more than eight inches high. But those I planted reached a height of two and a half feet although it took them twelve years to do so. Variety convexa, much used as hedge material, is broad spreading and it prunes well in case one wants to keep it fairly low. It could probably not be kept much below three feet and then it would be a rather stiff but handsome hedge. Some of the truly low forms are varieties compacta, stokes and hetzi, all with foliage similar to box. Probably the most miniature form of all is 'Kingsville Green Cushion.'

Yew (Taxus). There are no better subjects for foundation planting than yews, from which we may select several kinds to serve as ground covers. There are the low and widely spreading English yews (Taxus baccata). The varieties horizontalis, repandens, procumbens, as their names imply, are good subjects, and their eventual spread is considerable. Japanese yews (T. cuspidata) may be had in low-growing forms, especially variety nana. Some of the yews have succulent red berries which birds love, but if we or the birds are to enjoy those berries pruning should be done with forethought.

Hinoki cypress (Chamaecyparis obtusa). This well-beloved lacy evergreen has several prostrate forms such as the broad and low variety compacta, and the one with almost creeping branches, var. pigmaea.

Creeping mahonia (M. repens). Less than a foot high this plant has foliage suggestive of, but less leathery than, English holly and in May it produces pinkish-yellow flowers in spikes.

Fragrant sarcococca (S. hookeriana humilis). If one wishes to try a seldom seen shrublet which is a true ground cover, instead of the much-used pachysandra, periwinkle, or English ivy, one might consider this evergreen plant. It spreads by runners, has glossy narrow upright growing foliage on short stems and seldom reaches more than a foot in height. It may need to be placed where it receives some protection.

Creeping euonymus (E. fortunei coloratus or var. radicans). These ground-hugging vines are evergreen. The former, var. coloratus, has leaves which turn purplish bronze or reddish in autumn and winter. The better known variety, radicans, has smaller and more pointed leaves which remain green.

GROUND COVERING SHRUBS WHICH REQUIRE AN ACID SOIL

American yew (Taxus canadensis). Rough, sprawling evergreen shrub not often seen in cultivated gardens. Its chief virtue is that it does not care how deep the shade is.

Lowbush blueberry (Vaccinium angustifolium). Low and tiny-leaved deciduous shrub, red autumn color and whose berries are food for birds.

Box huckleberry (Gaylussacia). Similar to lowbush blueberry but evergreen.

Sand myrtle (Leiophyllum). Low evergreen shrub with little leaves and tiny blossoms in spring. The species L. lyoni is a prostrate grower.

Pachistima (P. canbyi) under a foot high, is evergreen with narrow leaves but inconspicuous flowers. Leaves reddish in winter.

GROUND COVERING PERENNIALS WHICH REQUIRE AN ACID SOIL

Oconee-bells (Shortia). Roundish leaves practically lie on the ground, somewhat like galax.

Galax. Florists use its leathery leaves. It too is close to the ground and loves to spread its carpet of leaves at the feet of rhododendrons.

Bunchberry (Cornus canadensis). If it can be made contented this is a charming ground cover with four-petalled white flowers like those on the flowering dogwood trees.

Flowering wintergreen (Polygala). Often seen colonized in the woods, this little plant has glossy evergreen leaves.

Partridge berry (Mitchella). A tiny trailer with roundish evergreen leaves and red berries.

Ferns and allied plants. Handsome ferns which sway in the breeze make fine ground covers. The royal, the cinnamon and lady-ferns are among those which need an acid soil for their best development. Ground-pine and ground-cedar will do well nowhere but in very acid soil.

Effective use of ground covers as a foundation planting: periwinkle, ivies, pachysandra and a group of low-growing yews

GROUND COVERS FOR BANKS AND SLOPES

Vines

Any of several vines would spread rapidly over the slopes. They must not however come in contact with any other plants lest they overrun them. This is especially true of Hall's honeysuckle. The vines will probably need drastic pruning, or the old woody stems cut out in late autumn, particularly clematis and silver lace vine, to keep them from making a wild tangle. Of course only one kind of vine would be used in a given location. Of the following vines only Virginia creeper and ivy will have no perceptible blossoms.

Virginia creeper. In the woods, on the beach almost anywhere. Red autumn color.

Akebia. Dainty foliage and curious small mauve flowers in May.

English ivy. One of the best in town or country.

Silver lace vine. Cream panicles in profusion in late summer.

Virgin's bower clematis. White flowers August, September.

Climbing hydrangea. White flowers, June, July.

Perennial pea (Lathyrus). Red, purple or white blossoms July-September.

Hall's honeysuckle. Yellowish and purple flowers June, July, aggressive.

Henry honeysuckle. Similar to above, less vigorous climber, flowers June, July.

Plantain-lily (Hosta). Those with huge swirling decorative leaves would cover a large area.

Shrubs

Drooping leucothoë (L. catesbaei). Graceful sprawling broad leaf evergreen whose branches swerve toward the ground.

Rose acacia (Robinia hispida). Hairy-stemmed unruly shrub with good foliage and sweet-pea blossoms, rose-lavender in May, June.

Shrub yellow root (Xanthorhiza). Lacy foliage, no noticeable bloom.

Flowering raspberry (Rubus odoratus). Coarse foliage but large single rose-purple blossoms in July.

Ferns

bead-fern, hay-scented fern, bracken, Christmas-fern.

GROUND COVERS WHICH FORM A CLOSE MAT OR CARPET OF COLOR WHEN IN BLOOM

Creeping Charlie (Lysimachia). Round foliage on creeping stems, yellow blossoms in June and July.

Gill-over-the-ground (Nepeta hederacea). Little round scalloped leaves which lie flat on the ground. Erect blue flower clusters.

Sedum. Several of the ground hugging and trailing sedums mostly with yellow or white flowers, spring, summer.

Carpet bugle (Ajuga reptans). This familiar and useful ground cover with its spikes of blue flowers in spring is a rapid spreader. Other species may have handsomer blossoms but the plants do not spread as much as carpet bugle.

Creeping veronica (V. repens). This is a moss-like creeper with rose or bluish blossoms in spring and summer. More rampageous is V. officinalis and V. filiformis, both excellent ground covers with tiny blue flowers.

Pearlwort (Sagina). Tufted velvety evergreen carpet, like moss.

Creeping bluets (Houstonia serpyllifolia). Tiny mats from which come strong blue blossoms in May.

Sweet woodruff (Asperula). Delicate little plants with masses of white flowers in May.

St. Johnswort (Hypericum calycinum). Shrublet under a foot high, evergreen or half so. Large single yellow blossoms July or August.

Creeping forget-me-not (Omphalodes). Blue or white flowers in April or May. Naturalizes easily.

GROUND COVERS NOT LISTED ABOVE

Bergenia (a saxifrage). Large leathery basal leaves, pink flower clusters in spring.

Cypress spurge (Euphorbia). Fluffy effect, linear leaves, umbels of yellow bracts, summer.

Day-lily (Hemerocallis). The dwarf kinds are charming and their fountains of narrow leaves cover the ground effectively. Blooming schedule can be arranged.

Creeping phlox (P. stolonifera). Cymes of violet-colored blossoms amid prostrate narrow-leaved foliage.

Epimedium. Dainty blossoms in many colors from several species rise slightly above foliage in spring.

May-apple (Podophyllum). Leaves like low green parasols rise over the woodland floor, white blossoms underneath, in spring.

Wild-ginger (Asarum). A woodland plant, glossy leaves under which lie brown bells practically on the ground in early spring.

Woodbine (Lonicera periclymenum). Fragrant trailer, cream blossoms between June and August.

GROUND COVERS BETWEEN STEPPING STONES

See suggestions on pages 79-80.

Narrow Strip in the Shade

There is often a narrow strip between house and walk or between two buildings where there is almost perpetual shade, though not deep and dank. Several ideas for clothing this narrow area may be considered. We may garden in the perpendicular with vines which clamber up into the sun to bloom there. We may grow wisteria with purple or white trusses, but provision must be made that the powerful stems do not undermine the shingles. Later to bloom will be silver lace vine (Polygonum aubertii) to be joined by starry white blossoms from a clematis vine such a C. paniculata. Another handsome vine is climbing hydrangea (H. petiolaris). Though somewhat slow to become established it will reward us with thick green growth and white flowers in open clusters in early summer. To clothe the ground at the feet of any of these we might be content with just periwinkle, pachysandra or ivy. Goutweed (Aegopodium podagraria var. variegatum), a green and white ground cover, spreads rapidly though invasively but endures any amount of shade.

Other ideas for the narrow strip in spring might be a composition of wild flowers and ferns, as for example: tiny crested iris, yellow, blue or white violets, bloodroot (Sanguinaria) with its white star flowers, maidenhair or Christmas-ferns, interspersed with wild oats (Uvularia) and its yellow drooping bells, and white-flowered barrenwort (Vancouveria), both content in much shade and blooming in late spring. Wild bleeding heart (Dicentra eximia) is well behaved, and keeps on blooming for a long while.

For summer bloom there is common speedwell (Veronica officinalis). Though coarse and spreading it takes lots of shade. Creeping dalibarda should bloom intermittently into September, its flowers like hepaticas and a foliage carpet of lustrous green. Musk plant (Mimulus moschatus), the hardy little trailer, produces yellow flowers for months.

For midseason and autumn bloom, nothing could be easier and more tolerant than plantain-lilies (Hosta). These are to be had in a dozen or more species and varieties but the dwarf forms with slender foliage might better fit the narrow strip. Beautiful effects may be achieved with tuberous begonias and their sensational flower forms and color ranges. They do not care for hot sun but they do need strong light. The easiest procedure with tuberous begonias is to purchase the plants and sink them in their pots into the soil. They are not winter hardy but they will bloom through the summer and into autumn.

The only annual which could be relied upon in continuous shade (though not dense) is the often mentioned Impatiens. It is studded with shades of scarlet, pink or white blossoms from summer until autumn. Then it may be brought into the house and will continue to bloom on the window sill.

The exotic tuberous begonia requires no sun, only strong light.

❖ 6 ❖

SHADE IN TOWN

City Back Yard in the Shade

The problem of shade grows more and more acute in our
city gardens, for encroaching tall buildings cast deep
shadows, and there is nothing to do but to find plants which
tolerate these conditions. The old lawn areas give way to
flagstone and brick paving, and delightful planting schemes
may be arranged in beds and borders planned for the purpose. Imagine a wall fountain, a pool, or a distinguished
piece of sculpture in a setting of living green things. A tree
in such a garden, as for example a ginkgo sapling, a honey
locust or flowering fruit tree adds to its beauty and helps
to afford a little privacy. Trees of denser foliage add difficul-
ties to our problems, for, with shade from buildings, and
overhanging shade as well, we run the risk of making the
garden so dusky that few plants will be happy there.

Conditions in city gardens are exceedingly variable and
many factors contribute to the causes of failure or success.
Plants which prosper in a neighbor's garden may languish
in ours due to uncontrollable conditions such as gasoline
fumes, excessive smoke, dust and soot, lack of fresh-air currents, or the shade from trees in an adjoining garden. A contented city gardener told me recently that over a period of

many years' experience, she had finally learned to reduce her failures to about 40 per cent. But I would not be writing this at all if I were not reasonably certain that, in obeying the rules, we can do as well or even better than that. Luxuriant bloom must not be expected in this garden, yet many flowering plants may be counted upon, though given mostly shade. Even without flowers, isn't a green garden worth striving for?

The special problems of a city garden—smoke and soot—are factors which many of the hardiest plants cannot endure. They clog the breathing pores and so interfere with their well being. Plants recommended for city gardens will stand a far greater chance of surviving under these conditions if given frequent hosings for the removal of soot. Too much water may be injurious, for the garden without much sun stands in danger of the soil becoming too damp and cold. Good drainage is certainly necessary and frequent cultivation of the soil for proper aeration will help to insure success.

Another damaging factor in city gardening is the lack of free currents of fresh air, caused by enclosing walls and fences. Community gardens, where barriers are let down, are able to overcome this difficulty. Where there are vine-covered lattice barriers, or hedges instead of fencing, the air is better. However, those who like their privacy will not be willing to remove their walls. Those with pent-house or roof gardens suffer from the opposite condition—too much wind and draught, which is also distasteful to plants.

Soil in the city back yard sometimes consists in large measure of hardpan or clay subsoil which originally came from the house foundations, or of cement or rubble which the masons have left. Over this there is a top layer of soil which may at one time have been rich and loamy, though now quite exhausted. It may never have been properly aerated or fertilized, it certainly has become impregnated with city gases and the drainage is probably poor. This sounds very hopeless, and so it is. In such a case the soil should be removed to a depth of two feet, and replaced by good soil, rich in organic matter. But this may be an exceedingly costly matter, aside from havoc wrought when all this material is dragged through the house. In such a predicament pot gardening may be a very effective solution.

In cases where the soil is not in a hopeless condition, it may be necessary merely to scrape off the sooty topsoil and remove it to a depth of four to six inches. Then turn over the soil to the depth of a foot or so, add rich top soil, and perhaps some commercial fertilizer, which is sold in bags, if barnyard manures are objectionable or difficult to procure. A sprinkling of ground limestone may be added but it should not come in direct contact with the manure. Lime should be avoided if rhododendrons and azalea are to be planted nearby. Here peat moss and sand may be incorporated with the soil. (*See* Chapter on Soils.)

Where shade in the city garden is occasioned not by a permanent obstruction (such as a building) but by shade from a deciduous tree, opportunities for planting are far greater. Many plants are content with summer shade if only they may have spring sun. This includes some of the early spring bulbs.

An all evergreen garden would be interesting for

ourselves and for the neighbors. Let us design a little garden which faces so that the sun shines upon it for a short while early or late in the day, with possibly a little reflected light from across the way. The shade is high, the light strong and the air is not heavy.

We assume that the owners of this back yard are not at all garden minded. They wish only to enjoy an extra room out of doors for relaxation, for entertaining their friends and for the pleasure of viewing a refreshing scene from the house windows. They follow today's trend with no attempt at a lawn. Instead they gradually turn a large part of the ground space into a paved area. They consider the possibilities of paving with brick, stone or tile. Less costly, though not as easy under foot are crushed shale, wood chips, tiny pebbles and—the cheapest of all—gravel. They consider a dining terrace at the house end, and space has no doubt been reserved for plantings.

Raised beds are effective and convenient. They may be fashioned of brick, hollow tile, cement blocks or one of the many compositions to be had today. Wooden, porcelain or masonry tubs skillfully planted could be placed at strategic points. Raised beds are particularly recommended for gardens where soil and drainage are poor. It does away with the trouble of removing sour soil and the laying of drain pipes.

We shall be very selective in our choice of living green things, choosing materials which are reliable under city conditions, and bearing in mind that this is both summer and winter garden.

The only needle leaf evergreen truly reliable in town is yew (Taxus), available in upright, dwarf and spreading

Spring in the city back yard

varieties. As for broad leaf evergreens Japanese holly (Ilex crenata) in its several forms is highly to be recommended. Its small glossy leaves are suggestive of boxwood. The casually drooping Leucothoë with its long oval leaves does well in town and is deep shade tolerant. Japanese andromeda (Pieris japonica) may not bloom too luxuriantly but its foliage is beautiful. Rhododendrons and azaleas are appropriate even though they may bloom rather shyly.

Privet is an excellent city plant, and although deciduous it may well keep its leaves most of the winter. Privet, planted bare-rooted, meaning no ball and burlap, is very reasonably priced and the best natured of plants anywhere. If not clipped, its white flowers in summer are effective.

As ground covers there are the indispensable Ajuga, Vinca, Pachysandra and English ivy. Several evergreen ferns should do well, especially Christmas-fern and the little polypodies.

As for color in this garden, the easiest procedure is to buy potted plants as the seasons progress from spring to autumn. Wax begonias and fuchsias have a long season of bloom, caladiums have distinguished foliage; and a fine showing of potted chrysanthemums will enliven the garden. All the potted plants will require less attention if they are sunk into the soil, pots and all, and whisked away when desired. Of all annuals, Impatiens is probably the only one which endures considerable shade. It lends itself well to pot culture and has a fine range of colorings.

The house plants will be delighted to come out of doors for an airing. Philodendron and the other vines will be so happy they would like to climb a tree. If the house plants are removed from their pots, the roots will probably grow and spread so recklessly that when autumn comes it will be difficult to stuff them back even into larger sized pots, and rigorous pruning may be too much for them. Therefore the plants are perhaps better left in their original pots, sunk into the earth, and returned indoors later.

Here we have the potentialities for a restful out-of-doors living room. With a gay umbrella (for privacy, not sunshine), comfortable chairs and a chaise-longue, our city garden becomes a summer resort.

A GROUP OF PLANTS FOR THE CITY GARDEN IN LIGHT CONTINUOUS SHADE

Needle-leaved Evergreen Shrub

Taxus cuspidata and its many forms—upright, spreading, dwarf

Broad-leaved Evergreen Shrubs

Azalea several species
Euonymus fortunei species
Ilex crenata and its upright or low varieties (Japanese holly)
Ilex glabra compacta (inkberry)
Leucothoë and its dwarf variety
Mahonia repens (creeping M.)
Pieris Japonica (Japanese andromeda)
Rhododendron (several species and preferably some of the dwarf hybrids, but bloom would be sparse)

Deciduous Shrubs

Acanthopanax (five-leaved aralia)
Azalea several species

Ligustrum (privet)

Other familiar shrubs may do well, particularly *sweet-shrub* (Calycanthus), *mock-orange*, *hydrangea*, *Kerria*, *Clethra* (sweet pepperbush), *Rhodotypos* (jetbead) and *Weigela*.

Perennials as ground covers and trailers

Ajuga (bugle)

Epimedium

Lysimachia (creeping Charlie)

Pachysandra

Sedum nevii, S. ternatum, others

Vinca minor (periwinkle)

Other Perennials

Many species and varieties of *plantain-lily* (Hosta). A surprising number of delicate wild flowers seem to do well in a shaded city garden, but soil conditions must be right. Some of these are wild *bleeding-heart*, *wild geranium*, *Canada mayflower* (Maianthemum), *wild sweet-William* (Phlox divaricata), *Virginia bluebell* (Mertensia) and *native violets*. When violet leaves grow too large and floppy they may be sheared and new ones will appear. Many of these plants are effective among ferns.

Ferns

Hay-scented-fern, *cinnamon-fern*, *interrupted-fern*, *Christmas-fern* and *polypody*. The last two are evergreen.

Bulbs and allied plants

Lily-of-the-valley, tiny *Iris cristata*, *Scilla*, both short and tall species. Other spring bulbs do well in the shade of deciduous trees, but may need replacement in a year or two. The small early-blooming bulbs seem to hold their own longer as a rule than the taller ones.

Vines

(see pages 219-223 for methods of clinging)

The best non-flowering vines are *Virginia creeper*, *Boston ivy*, *English ivy* and *wild grape*. Easy and reliable flowering vines are *silver lace vine* (Polygonum), *virgins-bower* (Clematis virginiana) and *Japanese or Chinese wisteria*. Unless they are allowed to climb where there is sun they may not throw out many blossoms.

Annuals and Potted plants

Very few annuals do well in a city garden in the shade, nor are they easily raised from seed there. Most city gardeners buy potted plants or seedlings. Probably the best annual would be *patience plant* (Impatiens). *Flowering tobacco* (Nicotiana) and *wishbone flower* (Torenia) often do well in town.

Wax begonia, *fuchsias* and *fancy-leaved caladiums* may be set out for summer and autumn color, and potted *chrysanthemums* would join them. No windy corners for the caladiums lest their delicate leaves be damaged.

A Few Comparatively Small Trees where there is Sun for part of the Day

Weeping willow
Hawthorne
Magnolia (M. soulangeana)
Thornless honey locust (Gleditsia triacanthos, especially var. 'Shademaster')
Fruit trees: *apple, pear, cherry, carmine crab-apple*
Note: [*Maidenhair-tree* (Ginkgo biloba). A young sapling would remain small enough for years and is one of the best of all city trees. An *Ailanthus* will do extremely well but would in time become very large. The standard tree for the city street is the *London plane* (Platanus acerifolia)].

Gardening in a window

Extract from a letter by Thomas Gray, the poet, to the Reverend Norton Nicholls. June, 1769.

"And so you have a garden of your own, and you plant and transplant, and are dirty and amused; are you not ashamed of yourself? Why; I have no such thing, you monster; nor ever shall be either dirty or amused as long as I live! My gardens are in a window . . . and they go to bed regularly under the same roof that I do, dear, how charming it must be to walk out in one's own garden, and sit on a bench in the open air with a fountain and a leaden statue and a rolling stone and an arbour! Have a care of sore throat though and the ague.''

Enormous strides have been made in recent years in acquainting us with an increasing variety of house plants which nurserymen and florists everywhere have to offer an interested public. Big foliage plants are playing a prominent role in the decorative schemes of not only the modern home but public buildings with their immense glass windows.

Explorers bring back from tropical lands fascinating plants many of which, happily for us, will flourish indoors. These handsome exotics come from Africa, from tropical America, the Pacific Islands and the Far East. Today the person is rare who does not have at least one foliage plant for its decorative potentialities, even though he has no particular gardening interests.

It is fortunate for us that most of the foliage plants on the market do not require sun. A north window or a room which receives a great deal of light will suit the plants discussed here. A few are even content in a dim room.

Much is being done these days in growing house plants under artificial light. This controlled sunshine may greatly increase one's success with certain flowering plants and foliage plants as well. The subject bears investigation but is a study in itself beyond the scope of this book.

I might mention that African violets (Saintpaulia) are popular as house plants, in a light but sunless window. New kinds are being produced in great variety and increasing interest is shown in the growing of these charming plants with their single or double violet-like blossoms in white, pink, blue and shades of purple. Use tepid water and do not wash the foliage. Moist atmosphere is beneficial.

I have selected some twenty foliage plants which have given me pleasure through the years. For simplification I have divided them into three categories—climbers, low growers and the dramatic.

The window gardener, especially if he be a city dweller, will probably not care to prepare his own soil, but will purchase his potted plants from the florist, nurseryman or other local dealer. However, when repotting time comes, it is essential that these plants be supplied with rich friable soil.

A SELECTION OF CLIMBING PLANTS

Many of these are usually grown in a pot which has a slab of tree bark inserted into the soil. Or a stake may be used covered with sphagnum moss wrapped about it or held in place by string or wire.

Cissus rhombifolia mandina (grape ivy). Well-known glossy-leaved climber or trailer with irregularly toothed leaves. Its relative *C. antartica* (kangaroo vine) has larger, saw-toothed leaves, and a less graceful carriage. However, this is easier to maintain than grape ivy and is in fact one of the most tolerant of all house plants. Grape ivy soil should be kept moist but not too wet, while the kangaroo vine should be drenched and be allowed to become almost dry again.

Philodendron, many species. Among the many plants of this genus, the heart-leaved vine (*P. oxycardium*) so well known to us all is perhaps the most amenable of all, requiring not even strong light, though preferring it. It trails, it grows up on a support and is happy enough in a container of water. Another species, *P. hastatum* with large waxy arrow-shaped leaves, will root as it climbs against a support. This plant is sometimes called elephant's ear or spadeleaf. Still another, a dramatic climber is *P. panduræforme*, often called fiddle leaf or horse head. It has large leathery leaves curiously formed. All three of these philodendrons like to be kept very moist, but *P. hastatum* should not be constantly wet.

Scindapsus aureus (ivy-arum, golden pothos). This climber has elongated heart-shaped leaves blotched with pale yellow, or in some varieties marked silvery white. Water only when soil becomes dry, then drench thoroughly. Sun or shade.

Syngonium podophyllum albolineatum (sometimes wrongly called variegated Nephthytis). Here is another of those very easy ones. Mine has lived for years apparently content without even repotting, though it needs frequent watering and makes great strides when given a periodic dose of fertilizer. These popular plants have acute arrow-shaped leaves with pale yellow markings carelessly splashed along the midrib. Some varieties have deep green edges, others are unmarked. Syngonium may be kept as a non-climber if, when the shoots reach out for support, they are cut off below the node and allowed to root in a container of water. They will keep growing in water or they may of course be pot planted.

SOME LOW-GROWING FOLIAGE PLANTS

Aglaonema modestum (Chinese evergreen). A familiar house plant with no outstanding distinction excepting its reliability. The long pointed almond-shaped leaves might at maturity reach twelve inches. In soil or in water it thrives in a light room and seems to resent only direct sunlight.

Caladium varieties (fancy-leaved caladium). These distinguished foliage plants have almost translucent leaves, delicate as tissue paper. The leaves are large and heart-shaped and the most frequently seen kind (candidum) has white foliage with green veining and edging. But there are many color combinations and named varieties. There are those with red and green color schemes, others delicate rose with green edge or pink and white forms. They grow from tubers and need the soil kept well moist.

Hedera helix (English ivy). As a house plant the common English ivy is less attractive than some of its many named varieties available today,

with their free branching habit and small foliage. These ivies need not necessarily climb but can of course form spreading, somewhat trailing or cascading plants. Moist but not wet soil, strong light, a weekly sponging of the foliage, spraying or even immersion is greatly beneficial.

Tradescantia fluminensis (wandering Jew, spiderwort). This familiar plant scarcely needs description. Small leaves green on both sides, trailing stems, it grows in water as well as in soil. It is easily maintained, preferring brightness rather than sun. One variety has its foliage striped yellow or white. The kind whose leaves are striped silver and white above and dark purple underneath is of a different genus, *Zebrina pendula*, also a good house plant.

A FEW PLANTS WITH LARGE DRAMATIC LEAVES

Fatshedera lizei. The name denotes the blending of two plants, Fatsia and Hedera. The foliage of this shrub-like hybrid resembles that of both parents, its large size from Fatsia and its form from Hedera. By pruning, the plant may be kept low and bushy. Fatsia, often called aralia, is also a popular house plant with even larger, deep lobed foliage. If low growth is desired, there is a dwarf variety (*Fatsia moseri*). Sun or shade for these plants. Do not keep too wet.

Ficus elastica (rubber-plant). An old time favorite come back into popularity. If content it may grow too tree-like for the small place, but its tolerance is remarkable. Variety decora is especially recommended with rather broader leaves than the common kind. A more unusual species is *Ficus lyrata* (fiddleleaf plant). Its huge leathery leaves are roughly oval or fiddle-shaped. Other forms are also available. Allow to become moderately dry between waterings.

Monstera deliciosa (sometimes called Philodendron pertusum; hurricane plant or splitleaf). This large leaf plant with slit, slashed or hole-bored foliage may reach enormous proportions, but when young the foliage is uncut. It is a curiously designed plant and popular. Keep it moist but not too wet.

Philodendron selloum (tree philodendron). Exotic, spreading, short-stemmed plant with large deeply lobed leathery leaves. Sun or shade. To be kept moist.

Schefflera actinophylla (Australian umbrella tree). A plant of charm and quality. Its stalks carry highly glossy leaves, like huge fingers. It may in time become a monstrous plant for indoors. Water thoroughly but only when the plant tends to grow dry.

(Other plants suitable as house plants are described in Part Two. They are pick-a-back plant; wax begonia; rex begonia; fuchsia and patience plant.)

SOME "DO'S" AND "DO NOT'S" FOR POTTED PLANTS IN A WINDOW

1. It is impossible to say how often to water house plants. The smaller the pot, the quicker the soil dries out. Even in heated apartments, plants seem to require less water in winter than in summer. Soil in clay pots dries out more quickly than in glazed ones. Plastic pots are proving themselves very moisture retentive. It is a good practice to submerge the pots in water at least once a week, allowing them to remain there until the bubbles have ceased to rise. In this way they receive a thorough soaking from the root tips to the surface of the soil. Never give your plants just a superficial watering. That rule applies to gardening anywhere, as every one certainly knows. At this time carefully spray or wash the leaves on both sides.

2. Plants may be set in jardinieres, but water must not be allowed to accumulate at the bottom, for this tends to supply the roots with enough water to rot them. Too much water in the soil prevents the roots from receiving the

necessary air. To overcome this, place an inverted bowl, or anything convenient, in the bottom of the container to raise the pot up above the water line. Plants which grow in either soil or water would not be injured by standing in moisture.

3. When watering from the top use enough so that it runs off through the hole in the bottom of the pot. Do not use ice cold water on your house plants. It disturbs their well being. See that water is slightly tepid. If the plants are occasionally to be left without care for a few days, they may be allowed to stand in a little water. This will take care of a possible drying out, when no one is there to tend them.

4. A satisfactory way to keep plants healthy is to arrange the pots in an attractive composition upon a long, narrow tray which is several inches deep and partially filled with small pebbles. A little water may be kept constantly in the bottom. This keeps the plants cool and moist without injuring the roots. It also humidifies the air. This tray may be placed on a window-ledge or a table directly in a light window. Do not crowd the plants too close together. Some people favor the use of humidifying devices to create the moisture which house plants appreciate. However, a container of water on the radiator may suffice to overcome the dry air indoors.

5. If a plant is sickly do not feed it with a diet of rich food. One never treats an invalid so. I know a woman who used to gather up all the ailing plants from the homes of her friends. When the plants were back to normal she returned them to their owners. She lost interest in them once they became vigorous. I do not know what magic she used, for

she did not seem to have any extraordinary ideas about plant culture. I wonder if optimism could have anything to do with success in gardening. It seems to me that the pessimist is always in trouble with his plants. Is this coincidence or is it some sort of unconscious philosophy?

6. In transplanting do not transfer the plant to a new pot which is more than one or two sizes larger than the one from which it was removed. The pot must be absolutely clean. Most plants seem to prefer a pot which is a little too small to one that is too large. Do not fill the earth to the very rim, otherwise watering from the top will be difficult. After transplanting, water thoroughly but do not keep the plants too wet. Because some of the fine roots may be destroyed in transplanting, do not be discouraged if your plant remains static for a week or two; it is merely readjusting itself and growing new roots.

7. Do not put oil on the leaves of your plants to increase their luster. This only clogs the pores and prevents proper breathing. Keep the leaves free from dust and soot, and the soil well aerated by gentle plowing up of the surface. There are materials to be had which, when sprayed or smoothed over the foliage, render it sparkling.

8. It is not necessary to have a hole at the bottom of the flowerpot if drainage is arranged for in some other way. This may be accomplished by placing crushed shells, or sand or gravel in the bottom of the pot. A layer of sphagnum moss will keep the soil from running into the drainage material, but watering must be done carefully. The pot with the hole is safer.

9. Plants do not like to be in a draught but they want

fresh air, and we must see that they have it daily (but no icy blasts).

10. Plants should not be given fertilizer when resting, only when growing. Some of the chemical fertilizers in tablet form may be used sparingly. They are imbedded into the earth as far from the roots as possible; dissolving slowly, a little with each watering, they gradually stimulate the plant. For small pots these tablets may be broken up and applied in small pieces. There are a number of chemical or organic fertilizers in powder or in liquid form. Never use more than the manufacturer recommends.

11. When plants are grown in water, it should be replenished as soon as it evaporates. Some advise changing the water completely every few weeks, others do so every few months. As long as the plants are thriving it is perhaps best not to disturb them.

12. Healthy house plants seldom become disease prone. One should, however, be prepared. In warm weather insects may attack, such as mealy bugs, red spider or other mites, therefore have ready your counteractent. (See page 21, Foes and Friends.)

Window Boxes in Town and Country

IN STRONG DAYLIGHT AT ANY SEASON EXCEPTING SEVERE WINTER

Sun is Not Necessary

Evergreen shrubs:
Dwarf forms of Taxus (yew)
Dwarf forms of Ilex crenata (Japanese holly)
Small globe arbor-vitae

Vines:
  English ivy, *Baltic* variety is one of the hardiest

IN STRONG DAYLIGHT IN SPRING, SUMMER AND AUTUMN
Sun is Not Necessary

Evergreen shrubs same as above.
Vines for trailing over front of box:
  English ivy
  Grape ivy (*Cissus*)
  Vinca major, some forms white-margined, strong trailer
  Vinca minor (periwinkle), a darker green with blue-violet flowers in
    spring
Sprawling House Plants:
  Tradescantia (wandering Jew)
  Tolmiea menziesii (pick-a-back-plant)

A FEW SUMMER-FLOWERING PLANTS
Varying Degrees of Shade

Begonia semperflorens (wax begonia), shades of red, pink, white
Fuchsia, magenta, purple, scarlet combinations, pink and others
Impatiens (patience plant) white, pink, salmon, shades of red
Lobelia erinus (edging lobelia), blue, violet, rose, crimson
Vinca rosea (Madagascar periwinkle), pink, white

(These plants are all discussed in Part II or in the section on
House Plants.)

"WHO'S WHO" IN THE SHADE

In the compilation of these lists a great many specialists have been consulted. In the last analysis, however, L. H. Bailey has been an unfailing guide. The scientific and popular names conform with those in his *Hortus Second*. Where popular names are omitted there I have resorted to other authoritative sources. In some cases where *Hortus* seems to overstate the height of certain plants, as they grow in our middle eastern States, I have, under advisement, reduced them to a more normal limit, yet many are still too high, or so it seems to me.

Although these lists are fairly comprehensive they do not pretend to be exhaustive. It is very possible that I have omitted certain desirable plants which other gardeners have grown successfully in shade. I have even reluctantly omitted a few favorites of my own, which my critics felt were not plants to endure shade permanently, such as creeping thyme, houseleek, rock cotoneaster and certain peonies. Among the doubtful ones were sand-myrtle and daphne cneorum, but I could not bring myself to discard these pleasant companions which always bloom so happily for me in half shade.

Any grave omissions on my part will I hope be reported by my readers for the good of the cause of gardening in the shade. There will no doubt be differences of opinion regarding cultural directions and blooming seasons, for these vary so according to locality. It is hardly possible fully to track down the potentialities of all plants for the shade, or to note their temperamental behavior and reactions under all circumstances. Here again comments from the reader will be welcomed.

The gardener knows of course that many of the plants in these lists will bloom in either sun or shade, and so these friendly beings stand ready to prove their versatility.

Evergreens are of interest the year round in a town·garden: Japanese holly (*Ilex crenata*), rhododendron, Japanese andromeda (*Pteris japonica*) and ivies.

✦◇✦

PART TWO

A DIRECTORY TO PLANTS

Their Native Habitat, Characteristics and Potentialities

✦✦

Because of uncontrollable factors—such as weather conditions,
the age of plants, and variations in locality—
the height of plants and their blooming seasons
can only be approximated.

✦✦

In using this directory it is suggested that the reader first consult
the INDEX where both common names and botanical ones are to
be found. This saves time in tracking down the category of the
particular plant whose biography one is seeking.

✦✦

See SHADE TABLE *in which degrees of shade are discussed:*
FULL · LIGHT · HALF *on page 7.*

All plants marked "Native" are suitable for the Wild Garden.
Plants marked "R" are suitable for the Rock Garden.

Patience plants (*Impatiens*) and wax begonias in bloom all summer

ANNUALS—SUMMER BEDDING—POTTING PLANTS

These plants are not winter hardy in our eastern seaboard middle Atlantic states. They must be set out each year when danger of frost is past.

AUCUBA japonica
(Japanese aucuba)

HEIGHT: 2-3 ft.
SOIL: moist, well drained
SHADE: light to full
REMARKS: not winter hardy north where it is much used as house plant or window box subject. May be put out of doors in warm weather. Good city plant. Where reliably hardy this can become a tall evergreen shrub. Several var., one spattered with "gold dust". Japan.

BEGONIA rex-cultorum
(rex begonia)

HEIGHT: to 2 ft.
SOIL: rich
SHADE: bright light
REMARKS: much used as a house plant. Grown primarily for colored foliage. Metallic silvery tones combined with lavender-pink, maroon, red-purple, red, green markings. Not winter hardy but may be set out of doors in warm weather.

BEGONIA semperflorens
(wax begonia)

COLOR: white, shades of red, pink, orange, salmon
HEIGHT: about 1 ft.
BLOOM: almost continuously
SOIL: loamy
SHADE: half to light
REMARKS: fibrous-rooted, single or double flowers. Window box, house plant, border, city garden.

BEGONIA tuberhybrida
(tuberous begonia)

COLOR: many shades, red, pink, yellow, salmon, orange, white
HEIGHT: 1 to 3 ft.
BLOOM: summer, autumn
SOIL: rich humus, sandy, loamy well drained moist
SHADE: light to full but not closed in deep shade. Must have plenty of air but no high winds
REMARKS: Many named varieties and forms resembling camellias, carnations, roses, hollyhocks, daffodils. The multiflora strain comprises plants with many small

single or double flowers rising on stems well above the small pointed-leaved foliage. Begonia evansiana is the only one which might be hardy out of doors if in a sheltered place and protected as far north as N.Y.C. It has many small flesh-colored or white flowers, grows to 2 ft. tall and blooms in July and August. It self sows. Far East.

FUCHSIA magellanica
COLOR: red, blue, purple, pink, white combinations
HEIGHT: variable
BLOOM: long season
SOIL: rich
SHADE: strong light, half shade, or more
REMARKS: In warm climates fuchsias are shrubs which may reach 20 feet in height. In the north fuchsias are used primarily as house or greenhouse plants to be brought out of doors in summer. There are many handsome hybrid forms. Mex. and S. Am.

IMPATIENS sultanii and I. holstii
(patience plant)
COLOR: orange, scarlet, crimson, rose, pink, white
HEIGHT: under 2 ft.
BLOOM: continuous

SOIL: good garden
SHADE: very little sun
REMARKS: Easily grown from seed, and cuttings will root in water. Good house plant or summer garden subject. Tropical Africa, Zanzibar.

LOBELIA erinus, R
(edging lobelia) and its varieties
COLOR: blue, white, pink, crimson
HEIGHT: 4-9 in.
BLOOM: all season
SOIL: good garden
SHADE: half
REMARKS: a low-growing form, dwarf or trailing. Good for edging or bedding. S. Africa.

LUNARIA annua (honesty)
COLOR: purple-lavender, blue, white
HEIGHT: 2 to 3 ft.
BLOOM: May, June
SOIL: sandy damp preferred
SHADE: light
REMARKS: biennial or annual. Effective silver disk seed pods. Good for dry bouquets. Eu. Asia.

MIMULUS tigrinus
(monkey-flower)
COLOR: red, yellow
HEIGHT: 1-1½ ft.
BLOOM: all season

SOIL: moist
SHADE: half
REMARKS: see also Mimulus under perennials.

NICOTIANA—several species
(flowering tobacco)
COLOR: rose, red, white
HEIGHT: 2-5 ft.
BLOOM: all season
SOIL: good garden
SHADE: half
REMARKS: sensitive to frost. N. alata grandiflora (affinis) is fragrant and has white flowers which are closed in the daytime and open at night. White flowers of N. sylvestris, fragrant, remain open in daytime. S. Amer.

TORENIA fournieri, R
(wishbone flower)

COLOR: blue, violet, yellow combinations
HEIGHT: to 1 ft.
BLOOM: all season
SOIL: moist
SHADE: half, protect from hottest sun
REMARKS: in Florida they are used as a substitute for pansies. Flowers tubular. Cochin-China.

VINCA rosea
(Madagascar periwinkle)
COLOR: rosy lavender, white
HEIGHT: 1-2 feet
SOIL: good garden
SHADE: half to light
REMARKS: grown as an annual, useful in window box, but high winds will blow away the blossoms. Glossy foliage. Madagascar.

AQUATICS

HARDY

ACORUS calamus (sweet flag)
DEPTH: in about 2 in. of water
SHADE: half
REMARKS: saber-like leaves; the variety variegatus has striped green and ivory leaves. Northern hemisphere.

ALISMA
(water-plantain)
COLOR: white
DEPTH: in shallow water (2 in.)
SHADE: half
REMARKS: branching spikes of flowers. U.S., Europe, Asia.

CALLA palustris
(water arum, wild calla)
COLOR: green outside, white inside
DEPTH: in few inches of water
BLOOM: June
SHADE: half
REMARKS: flower looks like calla-lily. Dense cluster of red berries in August. Native.

CALTHA palustris
(marsh-marigold)
See under Perennials.

IRIS versicolor
See under Bulbs and Allied Plants.

MENYANTHES trifoliata
(bogbean, buckbean)
COLOR: pink tinged
BLOOM: late spring
DEPTH: in shallow water
SHADE: half
REMARKS: creeping, fragrant flowers on stalks. Northern hemisphere.

NYMPHÆA—many species
(water-lily)
Some of these may be tried, but it is doubtful if they will bloom without sun most of the day.

They are worth growing for their leaves, which make decorative patterns on the water surface. Some are hardy, others are not. The pigmy lilies are effective in small ponds. Hardy and tropical kinds.

NYMPHOIDES peltatum
(floating-heart, water fringe)
COLOR: bright yellow
BLOOM: June-August
DEPTH: in shallow water (2-6 in.)
SHADE: half
REMARKS: small floating heart-shaped leaves. Europe, Asia, America.

NUPHAR advenum
(cow-lily, common spatterdock, yellow pond-lily)
COLOR: yellow, tinged green or brown
DEPTH: 12 in. under water
BLOOM: May
SHADE: half
REMARKS: leaves floating, 1 ft. long. Cup-shaped flowers, not very distinguished. Native.

PONTEDERIA cordata
(pickerel-weed)
COLOR: blue, upper lobes have two yellow spots

BLOOM: July-August
DEPTH: 12 in. under water
SHADE: half
REMARKS: easily grown, flowers on spikes, arrow-shaped leaves. Native.

SAGITTARIA sagittifolia
(old world arrowhead)

DEPTH: 18 in. in water
COLOR: white
BLOOM: summer
SHADE: half
REMARKS: leaves shaped like arrow heads. The double-flowered var. flore-pleno blooms longer. Tall spikes, white flower pom-poms. A native species S. latifolia also handsome. Eu. Asia.

SAURURUS cernus (lizards-tail)
COLOR: white
BLOOM: June-August
DEPTH: 2 in. under water, or damp ground
SHADE: half
REMARKS: flowers small fragrant, on spikes. Native.

TROPICAL

The tropical aquatics will not endure frost.

COLOCASIA antiquorum
(elephants-ear, imperial taro)

DEPTH: crowns not under water
SHADE: half
REMARKS: large, elongated, heart-shaped leaves on erect stems. Tropical effect. E. Indies.

EICHHORNIA crassipes
(water-hyacinth)

COLOR: lilac-blue
DEPTH: floating
BLOOM: summer
SHADE: half
REMARKS: orchid-like flowers in spikes. Increases rapidly, floats on water with bladdery leaf-stalks. Tropical America.

JUSSIÆA longifolia
(primrose-willow)

COLOR: yellow
BLOOM: summer
DEPTH: 2 in. of water
SHADE: half
REMARKS: attractive flowers like fragile single roses. There is a creeping species (repens) also desirable. Brazil.

MARSILEA drummondii (pepper-wort, four-leaf water clover)

HEIGHT: floating
DEPTH: crown not under water
SHADE: half
REMARKS: floating clover-like leaves. Australia.

MYRIOPHYLLUM proserpina-coides
(parrots-feather)

REMARKS: a plant most used in goldfish pools. Stems will live floating on the surface of the water, but will spread better if planted.

NYMPHÆA
(water-lily)
See under Hardy Aquatics.

BULBS AND ALLIED PLANTS

BEGONIA See under Annuals, etc.

CAMASSIA—all species (camass)
COLOR: purplish blue, dark blue, white, light blue
HEIGHT: to 3 ft.
BLOOM: May
SOIL: loamy, moist
SHADE: half, or among deciduous trees in high shade
REMARKS: somewhat like Scilla, but taller and handsomer. Plant about 5 in. deep, 5 inches apart in Sept. Native.

CHIONODOXA—all species, R
(glory-of-the-snow)
COLOR: blue, white, pink
HEIGHT: to 8 in.
BLOOM: early spring
SOIL: moist
SHADE: half, or shade of deciduous trees

REMARKS: plant about 3 in. deep, 4 in. apart in Sept. Asia Minor.

COLCHICUM—all species, R
(meadow-saffron, autumn-crocus)
COLOR: purple, rose, violet, white
HEIGHT: to 1 ft.
BLOOM: August or September, even Oct.
SOIL: loamy
SHADE: half
REMARKS: attractive in casual groups. Plant in July or August, tops 2 in. below surface, 6-9 in. apart. Do not disturb until they show signs of deterioration. Will bloom a few weeks after planting. Leaves appear the next spring, but die down before summer. N. Africa, Europe, Asia Minor.

CONVALLARIA majalis
(lily-of-the-valley)

COLOR: white
HEIGHT: to 10 in.
BLOOM: May
SOIL: moderately rich
SHADE: under deciduous trees
or light to full shade
REMARKS: flowers fragrant. Plant
1 in. deep, 5 in. apart. Europe,
Asia, N.E. America.

CROCUS—many species, R
(spring crocus)

COLOR: white, yellow, lilac,
orange, striped
HEIGHT: 3-6 in.
BLOOM: mid March to late April
SOIL: well drained
SHADE: among deciduous trees,
spring sun
REMARKS: first signs of spring.
Plant 3-4 in. deep, in Aug.-Sept.
Naturalized in U.S.A., Europe,
Asia.

DAFFODIL. See Narcissus.

ERANTHIS hyemalis, R
(winter aconite)

COLOR: yellow
HEIGHT: to 8 in.
BLOOM: very early
SOIL: good moist, a little lime if
soil is acid

SHADE: among deciduous trees
REMARKS: flowers like buttercups. Europe. Somewhat naturalized in America. Foliage disappears by July. Plant 3 in. deep
July, August.

ERYTHRONIUM—many species, R
(adders-tongue, trout-lily, dog-
tooth violet)

COLOR: yellow, violet, cream,
rose, mauve, orange, pink
HEIGHT: 10-18 in.
BLOOM: mid April-mid May
SOIL: loamy, gritty, moist, well
drained.
SHADE: light
REMARKS: foliage disappears soon
after flowering. Desirable in
almost any type garden. Western
species demand good drainage.
Plant Aug.-Sept. 3 in. deep, 6 in.
apart. Mostly native.

FRITILLARIA imperialis
(crown imperial)

COLOR: purplish, brick or yel-
low red
HEIGHT: to 3 feet
BLOOM: April
SOIL: rich, deep, well drained,
crown with ashes in winter
SHADE: half shade or shade of
deciduous trees

REMARKS: bell-shaped flowers. The tallest flower blooming so early in the season. Plant 5 in. deep, 6 in. apart in Aug. Persia.

FRITILLARIA meleagris (guinea-hen flower, checkered-lily)

COLOR: various shades checkered, striped and splashed with purple and maroon
HEIGHT: to 1 ½ ft.
BLOOM: April
SOIL: somewhat dry
SHADE: half or shade of deciduous trees
REMARKS: naturalizes well. Plant 3-4 in. deep, Sept.-Oct. Europe, Asia.

GALANTHUS in variety, R (snowdrop)

COLOR: white
HEIGHT: 3-5 in.
BLOOM: before spring
SOIL: well drained
SHADE: half, or among deciduous trees
REMARKS: plant with deciduous, not evergreen ground covers. Appears as snow melts. Does not like to be disturbed. Plant bulbs in Aug.-Sept. 3-4 in. deep, 3-4 in. apart. Europe, Asia.

IRIS gracilipes, R (Japanese crested Iris)

COLOR: pink-lilac, small
HEIGHT: to 10 in.
BLOOM: May
SOIL: moist, well drained, no lime
SHADE: deciduous trees, not dry or hot
REMARKS: grass-like foliage. It withstands more shade than the other dwarf iris excepting I. cristata and I. verna.

IRIS cristata, R (crested iris)

COLOR: blue
HEIGHT: under 6 in.
BLOOM: April, May
SOIL: woodland soil
SHADE: any of deciduous trees
REMARKS: increases rapidly. Native.

IRIS lacustris, R
Differs from Iris cristata in being lower, in fact this is the smallest of the native Iris (4 in. maximum). Light to half shade.

IRIS pumila
COLOR: yellow, violet
HEIGHT: almost stemless
BLOOM: May, June
SOIL: good garden

SHADE: of deciduous trees or half

REMARKS: rapid spreader, a bearded Iris. Russia, Asia Minor.

IRIS reticulata

COLOR: deep violet, orange touches

HEIGHT: usually a few inches

BLOOM: April

SOIL: good garden

SHADE: of deciduous trees or half

REMARKS: bulbous root. Fragrant. Some protection may be necessary. (The name reticulata is also given to a tall bearded iris.) Caucasus.

IRIS tectorum

(Chinese or Japanese roof I.)

COLOR: clear blue, white

HEIGHT: 1 ft.

BLOOM: May, June

SOIL: rich, not too dry

SHADE: deciduous trees or half

REMARKS: not too hardy north of N.Y.C. Sometimes temperamental. China.

IRIS verna, R

(dwarf iris, vernal iris)

COLOR: violet blue

HEIGHT: 4-6 in.

BLOOM: May

SOIL: acid preferably

SHADE: any except dense

REMARKS: fragrant, grows well with rhododendron, among rocks, on hillsides, in woodland. Native.

IRIS versicolor (blue flag)

COLOR: blue

HEIGHT: to 3 ft.

BLOOM: May-July

SOIL: moist or normal

SHADE: half

REMARKS: handsome and decorative. Native.

JONQUIL. See Narcissus.

LEUCOJUM vernum, R

(snowflake)

COLOR: white, tipped green

HEIGHT: to 1 ft.

BLOOM: early spring

SOIL: well drained

SHADE: half, or shade of deciduous trees

REMARKS: fragrant, plant 4 in. deep, 6 in. apart in early autumn. Do not disturb. Plant in groups, var. carpathicum has larger yellow tip bloom. Europe.

LILIUM canadense (meadow lily)

COLOR: orange-yellow to red, spotted brown

HEIGHT: to 5 ft.

BLOOM: June, July
SOIL: moist, well drained
SHADE: light to half
REMARKS: protect roots and
stems with undergrowth planting. Fine among azaleas in damp
peat or leaf-mould. Plant 6-8 in.
deep. Native.

LILIUM grayi (Gray's lily)
COLOR: red tinged yellow, spot-
ted purplish brown
HEIGHT: to 4 ft.
BLOOM: June, July
SOIL: any good
SHADE: half
REMARKS: graceful and of easy
culture. Plant 4 in. deep. Native.

LILIUM hansonii
COLOR: orange-yellow, spotted
purplish brown
HEIGHT: to 5 ft.
BLOOM: June
SOIL: any good
SHADE: half to light (not in full
sun)
REMARKS: fragrant. Plant 8-9 in.
deep. Japan.

**LILIUM leucanthum var. chlor-
aster** [centifolium]
(Chinese white lily)
COLOR: white tinged rose-
purple, greenish center marks
HEIGHT: 5-6 ft.
BLOOM: August
SOIL: sandy loam and leaf mould
SHADE: half
REMARKS: large, with sometimes
as many as twenty flowers to a
stem. Plant 9 in. deep.

LILIUM michauxii [carolinianum]
(Carolina lily)
COLOR: orange-scarlet, spotted
brown
HEIGHT: to 4 ft.
BLOOM: July
SOIL: dry, sandy
SHADE: half to light
REMARKS: similar to L. super-
bum but less hardy north. Plant
6 in. deep. Native.

LILIUM philadelphicum
(wild red lily, orangecup lily,
wood lily)
COLOR: orange-red, spotted with
purple
HEIGHT: to 3 ft.
BLOOM: June, July
SOIL: dry or moist
SHADE: light or half, border of
woods
REMARKS: one of our most beautiful native lilies. Plant 5 in.
deep.

LILIUM regale (regal lily)
COLOR: purple outside, white within, yellow at base
HEIGHT: 3-5 feet
BLOOM: June, July
SOIL: not particular
SHADE: half
REMARKS: fragrant, very easy. Plant 7 or 8 inches deep autumn or early spring. W. China.

LILIUM speciosum
(showy Japanese lily)
COLOR: white, rose tinged, rose spotted
HEIGHT: to 4½ ft.
BLOOM: late summer
SOIL: light, fertile sandy loam
SHADE: half to light
REMARKS: fragrant. Reflexed petals. Several var. Plant 6-8 in. deep in early spring. Mulch in early summer. Japan.

LILIUM superbum
(American Turks-cap lily)
COLOR: orange-scarlet, spotted brown
HEIGHT: 3-8 ft.
BLOOM: July
SOIL: rich, moist
SHADE: light open woodland, light to half
REMARKS: showy and handsome Plant 6 in. deep. Native.

LILIUM testaceum (Nankeen lily)
COLOR: apricot or nankeen yellow, often flushed with pink
HEIGHT: to 7 ft.
BLOOM: June-July
SOIL: sandy, loamy or ordinary garden
SHADE: half
REMARKS: well suited to pot culture. Fragrant, hybrid. Plant 4 in. deep. Europe.

LILIUM tigrinum (tiger lily)
COLOR: orange or salmon red, spotted purple-black
HEIGHT: to 4 ft.
BLOOM: July, August
SOIL: any good
SHADE: light
REMARKS: easily grown and beautiful, var. splendens recommended. Plant 6-8 in. deep. China, Japan, naturalized in part of U.S.

MUSCARI botryoides, R
(grape-hyacinth)
COLOR: blue, white
HEIGHT: to 1 ft., usually about 6 in.
BLOOM: April, May
SOIL: good, well drained
SHADE: open shade of deciduous trees
REMARKS: Plant 4 in. deep, 3 in.

apart in Sept.-Oct. 'Heavenly Blue' a handsome var. Attractive in groups. Colonizes. S. Europe.

NARCISSUS in many forms (narcissus, daffodil, jonquil)

COLOR: yellow, white and combinations
HEIGHT: to 1½ ft.
BLOOM: May, June
SOIL: well drained
SHADE: light to half
REMARKS: N. poeticus and others naturalize beautifully. Plant in September or October 4 in. deep, 6 in. apart. Europe.

ORNITHOGALUM umbellatum, R (star-of-Bethlehem)

COLOR: white, green margins
HEIGHT: 6 to 8 in.
BLOOM: April, May
SOIL: not demanding
SHADE: half
REMARKS: bulbous-rooted, grasslike leaves disappear in summer. Naturalizes well under trees, in grass. O. nutans has larger flowers and is taller. Med. regions.

SCILLA hispanica (Spanish bluebell)

COLOR: blue, white, pink tones
HEIGHT: to 15 inches
BLOOM: May
SOIL: good garden
SHADE: any except dense
REMARKS: good named varieties. The English bluebell (S. nonscripta) is similar but leaves are broader and plants multiply less rapidly. Plant 6 in. deep, 4-6 in. apart in early autumn. Spain, Portugal, Europe.

SCILLA sibirica, R (squill, bluebell, wood hyacinth)

COLOR: blue, white
HEIGHT: 6 inches
BLOOM: March, April
SOIL: well drained, loamy
SHADE: light, or shade of deciduous trees
REMARKS: naturalizes well. Plant 2 in. deep, 4 in. apart in September. Africa, Asia, Europe.

TULIPA, many species (tulips)

COLOR: in great variety
HEIGHT: 6-24 in.
BLOOM: April, May
SOIL: cool, rich, well drained
SHADE: half, or deciduous trees
REMARKS: The wild or species tulips do particularly well such as T. kaufmanniana, T. clusiana and others. These are small, lowgrowing and early bloomers. Plant Oct.-Nov.

FERNS

Of the many ferns available for planting in the shade, the following short list has been selected as representative of the principal genera and a few of their species which are more or less commonly found in our eastern states.

The varieties with a crown should be planted level with the surface of the ground, while those growing from underground root stocks should be planted just below the surface.

ADIANTUM pedatum
(maidenhair-fern)

HEIGHT: 10-20 in.
HABITAT: rich loamy humus soil
SHADE: any except dense
REMARKS: delicate, lacy fronds. Black wiry stems, spreading by root stocks. One of our most beautiful ferns, easily cultivated.

ASPLENIUM trichomanes and other species, **R**
(maidenhair spleenwort)

HEIGHT: 2-8 in.
HABITAT: moist or dry rock ledges
SHADE: any
REMARKS: delicate and lacy, individual blade somewhat like maidenhair-fern. It forms charming rosettes against the rocks. Evergreen.

ATHYRIUM filix-femina
(lady-fern)

HEIGHT: 16-32 in.
HABITAT: moist acid woods and thickets
SHADE: any except dense
REMARKS: charming, but tatters mid season unless in right location.

BOTRYCHIUM virginianum
(rattlesnake-fern)

HEIGHT: 8-24 in.
HABITAT: moist woodland preferably
SHADE: any except dense
REMARKS: a stalk of tiny grape-like spore cases in late spring.

CAMPTOSORUS rhizophyllus, R
(walking-fern)

HEIGHT: 4-12 in.
HABITAT: sheltered limestone ledges and cliffs
SHADE: any except dense
REMARKS: difficult; sword-shaped small leaves, the ends of which grow very pointed and root after they touch the earth

producing a new plant in late summer. Evergreen.

DENNSTAEDTIA punctilobula
(hay-scented-fern)

HEIGHT: 16-36 in.
HABITAT: well drained, dry or moist acid
SHADE: any except dense, also sun
REMARKS: effective massed in the open but rampageous.

DRYOPTERIS filix-mas
(male-fern)

HEIGHT: 12-36 in.
HABITAT: moist rich soil
SHADE: any
REMARKS: nearly evergreen. Conservationists advise not to take from the wild.

DRYOPTERIS goldiana
(giant woodfern, Goldies-fern)

HEIGHT: 20-40 in.
HABITAT: rich cool humus soil
SHADE: any
REMARKS: one of our largest wood ferns, urn form, dramatic. Do not take from the wild.

DRYOPTERIS hexagonoptera
(southern beech-fern, broad beech-fern)
HEIGHT: 8-16 in.

HABITAT: wooded and rocky slopes
REMARKS: the general shape of the leaf is equilateral triangular. Grows from root stocks in rows, spreading.

DRYOPTERIS spinulosa intermedia (evergreen woodfern)

HEIGHT: 16-32 in.
HABITAT: woods, shaded rocky slopes
SHADE: any
REMARKS: evergreen clusters, good slope cover. Florists' "fancy fern."

LYCOPODIUM complanatum
(ground-cedar)

HEIGHT: 2-4 in.
HABITAT: very acid, dry soil, open woods, thickets, rocky slopes
SHADE: any
REMARKS: grows in rows from root stocks. A club moss. Must have proper soil conditions.

LYCOPODIUM obscurum
(ground-pine)

HEIGHT: to 8 in.
HABITAT: woodland not rich, acid
SHADE: any
REMARKS: tree-like growth.

Spreads by root stocks. A club moss. Must have proper soil conditions.

ONOCLEA sensibilis
(bead-fern, sensitive-fern)
HEIGHT: 12-30 in.
HABITAT: wet or moist soil. Will stand some acidity.
SHADE: any excepting deep
REMARKS: rapid spreader, beautiful bronzy-pink crosiers. Grows in rows by root stocks. "Bead" refers to bead-like fertile pinnules. Sensitive only to frost or injury. Apt to become weedy, rampageous.

OSMUNDA cinnamomea
(cinnamon-fern)
HEIGHT: 30-60 in.
HABITAT: moist acid peaty soil
SHADE: any
REMARKS: only the fertile fronds wither early. Large exposed root stocks. Grows in clusters. Needs space, often called "fiddle heads."

OSMUNDA Claytoniana
(interrupted-fern)
HEIGHT: 30-60 in.
HABITAT: moist wooded slopes, swamp margins, loamy soil in open thickets, neutral or slightly acid soil. Moist or dry.

SHADE: any
REMARKS: makes large frond clusters. The interrupted space seen near middle of frond is caused by the withered-away clusters of sporangia. This is the only Osmunda which does well in dryer soil. Needs space. Handsome.

OSMUNDA regalis (royal-fern)
Height: 20-60 in.
HABITAT: moist or swampy, peaty acid soil
SHADE: any excepting dense
REMARKS: grows in clusters. Fronds when uncurling are beautiful pale pink and yellow. Tall, dramatic. Needs space.

POLYPODIUM vulgare, R
(polypody, rockcap)
HEIGHT: 4-12 in.
HABITAT: on dry rocks and ledges, wooded banks
SHADE: any
REMARKS: grows on flat shelves in rocks and ledges. Evergreen. Attractive for rock garden. Needs humus.

POLYSTICHUM acrostichoides
(Christmas-fern)
HEIGHT: 12-30 in.

HABITAT: ravines and thickets, dry or moist soil not rich

SHADE: any

REMARKS: good slope cover, dark green leathery evergreen fronds. Clusters, easy and desirable, most useful.

PTERETIS nodulosa (ostrich-fern)

HEIGHT: 20-80 in.

HABITAT: rich moist swampy soil

SHADE: any excepting dense

REMARKS: produces clusters of fronds, vase-like in form. Rapid spreader by underground root stocks. Plumelike fronds. Dramatic.

PTERIDIUM aquilinum (bracken, brake)

HEIGHT: 16-32 in.

HABITAT: sterile, usually acid soil, moist or dry

SHADE: any, or full sun

REMARKS: grows along root stocks in rows. Large, coarse, good distant ground cover, aggressive.

HERBACEOUS PERENNIALS FOR VARYING DEGREES OF SHADE

ACONITUM fischeri

COLOR: blue or white

HEIGHT: 3-5 ft.

BLOOM: autumn

SOIL: rich

SHADE: light

REMARKS: naturalizes easily, attractive leaves. Asia. The form wilsonii has violet flowers.

ACONITUM napellus (true monkshood)

COLOR: blue

HEIGHT: to 4 ft.

BLOOM: July-August

SOIL: rich

SHADE: light

REMARKS: varieties have white or blue and white flowers. Var. sparksii is much used. Europe.

ACONITUM uncinatum (wild monkshood)

COLOR: blue

HEIGHT: to 5 ft., partially climbing

BLOOM: June-September

SOIL: rich, moist

SHADE: light, prefers no sun

REMARKS: needs staking, or allowed to climb. Native.

ACTÆA alba, R
(white, baneberry, cohosh)

COLOR: white racemes
HEIGHT: to 1½ ft.
BLOOM: April-June
SOIL: rich woodland
SHADE: any
REMARKS: China-white berries in August. Native.

ACTÆA rubra
(red baneberry)

COLOR: white racemes
HEIGHT: to 2 ft.
BLOOM: April-June
SOIL: rich woodland
SHADE: any
REMARKS: bright red berries. Native.

ÆGOPODIUM podagraria, var. variegatum
(goutweed, bishops-weed)

COLOR: white
HEIGHT: to 14 in.
BLOOM: June
SOIL: any garden, preferably moist
SHADE: full
REMARKS: spreading ground cover near wall or under trees. White-margined foliage, aggressive. Europe, naturalized in N. Am.

AJUGA genevensis, R
(Geneva bugle)

COLOR: blue, white, rose var.
HEIGHT: to 14 in., but usually under 8 in.
BLOOM: May, June
SOIL: good garden
SHADE: almost any
REMARKS: less spreading than A. reptans, flowers on erect stems. Border, rocks, edging, var. brockbanki has tall blue spikes in summer. Europe.

AJUGA pyramidalis, R
(metallic bugle)

COLOR: gentian blue
HEIGHT: flowers on 9 in. stems
BLOOM: May, June
SOIL: good garden
SHADE: almost any
REMARKS: does not spread rapidly like the var. reptans. Metallic-green wrinkled leaves. Var. metallica crispa recommended. Europe.

AJUGA reptans, R (carpet bugle)
COLOR: blue, purple or white
HEIGHT: to 1 ft., usually 3-4 in.
BLOOM: May, June
SOIL: any ordinary
SHADE: any
REMARKS: rapid creeper, glossy

leaves, var. alba less spreading, good for shady slopes, ground cover, others with bronze, purple leaves. Europe.

ANCHUSA myosotidiflora. See Brunnera.

ANEMONE alpina, R
COLOR: creamy inside, outside purple
HEIGHT: to 1 ½ ft.
BLOOM: May-June
SOIL: rich, loamy
SHADE: half to light
REMARKS: flowers few but large. Europe.

ANEMONE apennina
(apennine windflower)
COLOR: sky blue
HEIGHT: to 9 inches
BLOOM: March, April
SOIL: woodland
REMARKS: naturalizes beautifully under tall trees. Tuberous-rooted. Italy. A. blanda from Asia Minor is similar.

ANEMONE canadensis, R
(meadow anemone)
COLOR: white
HEIGHT: to 2 ft.
BLOOM: May-August
SOIL: in rich leafy soil it may become too rampageous

SHADE: to full
REMARKS: spreading, attractive among ferns and rocks. Native.

ANEMONE japonica
(Japanese anemone)
COLOR: purplish, red, rose, white
HEIGHT: to 3 ft.
BLOOM: September to frost
SOIL: rich garden
SHADE: half to light
REMARKS: good for cutting, borders, under trees in cultivated ground. Japan, China.

ANEMONE nemorosa, R
(European wood anemone)
COLOR: white purplish, blue, rose
HEIGHT: to 8 in.
BLOOM: April-May
SOIL: rich sandy loam
SHADE: half
REMARKS: 'Royal Blue' is a recommended form. Europe, Siberia.

ANEMONE sylvestris, R
(snowdrop anemone)
COLOR: white
HEIGHT: to 1 ½ ft.
BLOOM: May-June
SOIL: rich garden
SHADE: light to half

REMARKS: spreader. Among rocks, border. Fragrant. Europe, S.W. Asia.

ANEMONELLA thalictroides, R
(rue anemone)

COLOR: whitish or pinkish
HEIGHT: 5 or 6 in. average
BLOOM: March-June
SOIL: light, rich woodland
SHADE: in thin woods
REMARKS: plant in masses. Native.

AQUILEGIA, many forms
COLOR: blue, purple, white, pink
BLOOM: spring, summer
HEIGHT: to 3 ft.
SOIL: light, humus, well drained
SHADE: half
REMARKS: desirable. Long blooming season may be arranged.

AQUILEGIA canadensis, R
(common American columbine)

COLOR: yellow and red
HEIGHT: to 2½ ft.
BLOOM: May-June
SOIL: light sandy loam
SHADE: light shade of deciduous trees
REMARKS: for borders, rock garden, and wild. Native.

AQUILEGIA vulgaris, R
(European columbine)

COLOR: blue, purple, white, rose, maroon
HEIGHT: to 2½ ft.
BLOOM: May to July
SOIL: light sandy loam
SHADE: half
REMARKS: the spurs are knobbed and much incurved. Europe, Siberia.

ARENARIA verna, R
(sandwort)

COLOR: white
HEIGHT: to 3 in.
BLOOM: summer
SOIL: good garden
SHADE: half
REMARKS: good between joints of stone paths. Var. cæspitosa makes moss-like patches. Europe, America.

ARISÆMA triphyllum
(Jack-in-the-pulpit, Indian turnip)

COLOR: green with purplish tinges
HEIGHT: to 3 ft.
BLOOM: May
SOIL: moist woods
SHADE: any
REMARKS: scarlet berries in early

summer. Plant singly among ferns. Native.

ARUNCUS sylvester [Spiræa aruncus]
(goats-beard)
COLOR: white
HEIGHT: to 7 ft.
BLOOM: June-July
SOIL: moist
SHADE: half
REMARKS: desirable border plant, showy panicles. Like Astilbe. Native, Europe, Asia.

ASARUM canadense, R
(wild-ginger)
COLOR: brown
HEIGHT: to 1 ft., usually lower
BLOOM: May
SOIL: rich, moist
SHADE: light to deep
REMARKS: heart-shaped leaves, ground cover. Bell-shape flowers lying close to ground. Species europaeum with handsome foliage is recommended, it is also evergreen. Native.

ASPERULA odorata, R
(sweet woodruff)
COLOR: white
HEIGHT: to 8 in.
BLOOM: May, June
SOIL: loamy, moist
SHADE: light

REMARKS: naturalizes well, increases rapidly, carpeting, edging, herb garden. Europe, Asia.

ASTER alpinus, R
(rock aster)
COLOR: violet, pink, white
HEIGHT: to 2 ½ in.
BLOOM: May-June
SOIL: ordinary
SHADE: half
REMARKS: single daisy-like flowers for rock garden or border. Native, Europe, Asia.

ASTER cordifolius
(blue wood aster)
COLOR: violet or blue
HEIGHT: to 5 ft.
BLOOM: September-October
SOIL: almost any
SHADE: half
REMARKS: wild garden only, somewhat weedy. Arching tiny flowers. Native.

ASTER divaricatus [corymbosus]
(white wood aster)
COLOR: white
HEIGHT: to 2 ½ ft.
BLOOM: autumn
SOIL: tolerates dry soil
SHADE: light to full
REMARKS: wild garden only, too weedy elsewhere. Native.

ASTER novi-belgii
(New York aster)

COLOR: bright blue-violet
HEIGHT: to 3 ft.
BLOOM: September, October
SOIL: likes moisture
SHADE: half
REMARKS: sometimes called Michaelmas daisy. Eu. origin.

ASTILBE species and hybrids.
COLOR: pastel pinks, white and red shades
HEIGHT: 4 inches to 3 feet
BLOOM: June, July, August, September
SOIL: rich, moist, well drained
SHADE: half
REMARKS: The species below is the only native one. All others are of Far Eastern origin, some of which have been intercrossed to produce many fine named varieties.

ASTILBE biternata
(blue-ridge astilbe, false spirea)

COLOR: yellowish white
HEIGHT: to 6 ft.
BLOOM: June
SOIL: moist
SHADE: half
REMARKS: border, good in masses, others blooming later have different colorings. Native.

BERGENIA cordifolia (A saxifrage)
COLOR: rose, lilac, purple, white
HEIGHT: to 20 inches
BLOOM: April, May
SOIL: rich, moist
SHADE: light to half
REMARKS: large leathery basal, evergreen leaves. Rockledges, front border, ground cover. Withstands city conditions. Species crassifolia has taller flower panicles. Siberia.

BRUNNERA macrophylla [Anchusa myosotidiflora]
(Siberian bugloss)

COLOR: blue
HEIGHT: to 1 ½ ft.
BLOOM: May-June
SOIL: good garden, moist
SHADE: half
REMARKS: coarse heart-shaped leaves. Flowers somewhat like forget-me-not. Siberia, Caucasus.

BUPHTHALMUM speciosum
(showy ox-eye)

COLOR: yellow
HEIGHT: to 4 ft.
BLOOM: June, July
SOIL: good garden
SHADE: light
REMARKS: large daisy-like flowers, bold, free, showy, good mass effect. S. Europe, W. Asia.

CALTHA palustris
(marsh-marigold)

COLOR: yellow
HEIGHT: to 2 ft.
BLOOM: April, May
SOIL: moist or in shallow water
SHADE: half
REMARKS: though naturally a swamp and marsh plant it will grow in the garden in rich moist soil. Native.

CAMPANULA carpatica, R
(Carpathian harebell or bellflower)

COLOR: bright blue to white
HEIGHT: to 1½ ft., usually 8-10 in.
BLOOM: summer
SOIL: garden
SHADE: half
REMARKS: looks well among rocks, as edging. E. Europe.

CAMPANULA latifolia
(great bellflower)

COLOR: purplish-blue
HEIGHT: to 4 ft.
BLOOM: June, July
SOIL: rich well-drained loam
SHADE: light
REMARKS: large fine flowers, several var. Attractive in wild garden also. Europe, Asia.

CAMPANULA portenschlagiana
[muralis], R (wall harebell, Dalmatian bellflower)

COLOR: blue-purple
HEIGHT: to 9 in.
BLOOM: June, July
SOIL: good garden
SHADE: half
REMARKS: lovely on wall among rocks, good edging. Dalmatia.

CAMPANULA rotundifolia, R
(bluebell, harebell)

COLOR: bright blue, white
HEIGHT: to 1½ ft.
BLOOM: all summer
SOIL: good garden
SHADE: light, half
REMARKS: identical with bluebell of Scotland. Delights in rocky crevice where it will cascade down. Europe, Asia, N. America.

CARDAMINE pratensis, R
(ladies-smock, cuckoo-flower)

COLOR: pink, white
HEIGHT: 1 to 1½ ft.
BLOOM: June
SOIL: woodsy, moist, cool
SHADE: light
REMARKS: attractive along creek or spring. Will stand drier places. Europe, northern U.S.

CERATOSTIGMA plumbaginoides, R (plumbago)

COLOR: deep intense blue
HEIGHT: to 1 foot
BLOOM: August-Sept.
SOIL: well drained loam
SHADE: half
REMARKS: border, edging. Starts growth later than most perennials. China.

CHELONE glabra
(white turtle-head, snake-head)

COLOR: white and pinkish
HEIGHT: to 3 ft.
BLOOM: July, August
SOIL: moist, rich
SHADE: half
REMARKS: effective in masses. Native.

CHELONE lyoni (turtle-head)
COLOR: rose-purple
HEIGHT: to 3 ft.
BLOOM: August
SOIL: moist, rich preferably
SHADE: half to light
REMARKS: glossy foliage. Flowers on spikes, good border plant. There is a dwarf form. Native.

CHIMAPHILA maculata, R
(pipsissewa, spotted wintergreen)
COLOR: white

HEIGHT: to 10 in., usually less
BLOOM: June-July
SOIL: dry, acid, woodsy. Pine or hemlock leaf mulch is beneficial. Must have right soil conditions
SHADE: light to full
REMARKS: evergreen leaves flat to the ground have white markings. Native.

CHIMAPHILA umbellata, R
(pipsissewa)
COLOR: white, pink center
HEIGHT: to 10 in., usually less
BLOOM: June-July
SOIL: same as C. maculata
SHADE: light to full
REMARKS: evergreen leaves do not have white markings like maculata. Europe, Japan, Native.

CHIOGENES hispidula, R
(creeping snowberry)
COLOR: tiny, white, bell shaped
HEIGHT: creeping
BLOOM: May-June
SOIL: cool, damp, mossy or peaty acid
SHADE: light
REMARKS: evergreen dainty member of heath family. Shiny white berries. Must have right soil conditions. Native.

CHRYSANTHEMUM arcticum, R
(Arctic chrysanthemum, Arctic daisy)
COLOR: white, pink, others
HEIGHT: to 15 in.
BLOOM: autumn
SOIL: good garden
SHADE: half
REMARKS: hardy, dark green foliage. Other low growing kinds also. Arctic regions.

CHRYSOGONUM virginianum, R
(golden-star)
COLOR: yellow
HEIGHT: 6-10 in.
BLOOM: spring, summer
SOIL: loamy
SHADE: light, dec. woods
REMARKS: small daisy-like flowers. Native.

CIMICIFUGA racemosa
(black cohosh, black snakeroot, bugbane)
COLOR: white
HEIGHT: to 8 ft.
BLOOM: July-August
SOIL: moist, rich
SHADE: light open to full
REMARKS: racemes on long spikes, looks well against dark background. Native.

CIMICIFUGA simplex (Kamtschatka bugband or snakeroot)
Similar to above, but lower growing and from Kamtschatka. It grows to 3 ft., blooming in autumn. An Asian species, C. davurica is also recommended growing to 5 ft. in Aug.-Sept.

CLAYTONIA virginica, R
(spring beauty)
COLOR: white with pink hairline stripes
HEIGHT: to 1 ft.
BLOOM: earliest spring
SOIL: leaf mould
SHADE: open shade under deciduous trees
REMARKS: dainty, charming, delicate. Native.

CLEMATIS. See under Vines.

CLINTONIA borealis (blue-bead)
COLOR: greenish yellow
HEIGHT: to 1 ft.
BLOOM: June, early July
SOIL: acid, moist, sandy, peaty
SHADE: any, even under evergreens
REMARKS: minute lily-like flowers terminate the stalk, leaves similar to lily-of-the-valley. Blue berries in summer. Native.

CLINTONIA umbellata
(speckled clintonia)
COLOR: white with brownish
tiny specks
HEIGHT: to 1 ft.
BLOOM: May-June
SOIL: acid, moist, sandy, peaty
SHADE: any
REMARKS: black berries. Native.

CONVALLARIA (lily-of-the-valley).
See Bulbs.

COPTIS groenlandica (goldthread)
COLOR: white
HEIGHT: to 6 in.
BLOOM: May-August
SOIL: damp, acid, peaty
SHADE: any
REMARKS: must have right soil
conditions. Evergreen ground
cover. Native. Other Coptis
species are also recommended.

CORNUS canadensis (bunchberry)
COLOR: white
HEIGHT: to 9 in., usually about
6 in.
BLOOM: May
SOIL: damp, cool, acid
SHADE: any
REMARKS: ground cover sub
shrub. Does not bloom its best in

deep shade. Red berries late
summer. Difficult to establish.
Native.

CORYDALIS lutea, R (fumitory)
COLOR: pale yellow
BLOOM: May to August
HEIGHT: 8 to 12 in.
SOIL: dry, well drained
SHADE: half
REMARKS: fern-like leaves, self
sowing, border, wall. S. Europe.

CYMBALARIA muralis [Linaria], R
(Kenilworth ivy)
COLOR: lilac-blue, rose, white
HEIGHT: long trailing and root-
ing at joints
BLOOM: all season
SOIL: ordinary
SHADE: light
REMARKS: a delicate vine-like
trailer attractive in chinks in a
wall. Not fully hardy north.
Europe, nat. in U.S.

CYPRIPEDIUM acaule, R
(pink lady-slipper, mocassin-
flower)
COLOR: sepals and petals green-
ish-brown, lip rose, veined
darker
HEIGHT: to 10 in.

BLOOM: May, June
SOIL: dry or moist, acid, woodsy, good drainage
SHADE: any
REMARKS: must have right soil conditions. Difficult. Native.

CYPRIPEDIUM calceolus pubescens, R (yellow lady-slipper)

COLOR: yellow, veined purple
HEIGHT: to 16 in.
BLOOM: June-July
SOIL: good garden, or woodland moisture
SHADE: among deciduous trees
REMARKS: small fragrant flowers. Native. C. japonicum and C. macranthum are also good.

CYPRIPEDIUM reginæ [C. spectabile], R (showy lady-slipper)

COLOR: rose and white
HEIGHT: to 2 ft.
BLOOM: June
SOIL: moist but not wet, woodsy
SHADE: light to full
REMARKS: handsome, large flowers. C. arietinum and candidum, are also recommended. Native.

DALIBARDA repens, R
(creeping dalibarda)

COLOR: white
HEIGHT: 3 to 4 in.

BLOOM: June-September, irregularly
SOIL: deep fibrous
SHADE: any
REMARKS: green, glossy carpet. Flowers resemble small hepatica. Native.

DELPHINIUM tricorne

COLOR: blue, lilac, lavender to white
HEIGHT: 1-3 ft.
BLOOM: May
SOIL: deep, rich, well drained
SHADE: half, no more
REMARKS: foliage dies down in midsummer. Native.

DENTARIA diphylla, R
(toothwort, crinklefoot)

COLOR: white
HEIGHT: 6 to 12 in.
BLOOM: spring
SOIL: rich woodland
SHADE: half
REMARKS: handsome in masses. Foliage dies down in summer. Native.

DICENTRA canadensis, R
(squirrel corn)

COLOR: greenish white, tinged purple
HEIGHT: 5-12 in.

BLOOM: April, May
SOIL: rich
SHADE: under deciduous trees
REMARKS: gray-green fern-like foliage, which disappears after flowers fade. Native.

DICENTRA cucullaria, R
(Dutchmans-breeches)

COLOR: cream, tipped with yellow
HEIGHT: to 10 in.
BLOOM: April, May
SOIL: loose, fibrous, wood
SHADE: under trees, not dense
REMARKS: foliage disappears soon after flowers fade. Native.

DICENTRA eximia, R
(wild bleeding-heart, fringed bleeding-heart)

COLOR: pink or rose
HEIGHT: to 18 in.
BLOOM: all summer
SOIL: good garden or woodland
SHADE: any, excepting dense
REMARKS: effective foliage until frost. Native.

DICENTRA spectabilis, R
(bleeding-heart)

COLOR: pink, rosy-red
HEIGHT: to 3 ft.

BLOOM: May, June
SOIL: good garden, not too rich
SHADE: light
REMARKS: if given space and moisture foliage will remain attractive until late summer. Japan.

DIGITALIS ambigua [D. grandiflora, D. ochroleuca]
(yellow foxglove)

COLOR: yellowish marked with brown
HEIGHT: to 3 ft.
BLOOM: June-July
SOIL: good garden
SHADE: light to half
REMARKS: good border plant. Europe. W. Asia.

DIGITALIS purpurea and its forms
(common foxglove)

COLOR: purple, white, rose, pink
HEIGHT: to 4 ft.
BLOOM: June, July
SOIL: good garden
SHADE: light to half
REMARKS: perennial or sometimes self-sowing biennial. In England this is a common wild flower. Excelsior hybrids recommended. W. Europe.

DODECATHEON meadia, R
(shooting star, American cow-slip)
COLOR: rose or white
HEIGHT: 8-20 in.
BLOOM: May, June
SOIL: well drained, cool, and gritty
SHADE: half, light
REMARKS: flowers like small cyclamen. Other species are also useful in half or light shade. Native.

DORONICUM plantagineum
(leopards-bane)
COLOR: yellow
HEIGHT: to 5 ft.
BLOOM: May-June
SOIL: rich loam
SHADE: half
REMARKS: other species also. Yellow disk, yellow ray. Good for cutting, but somewhat coarse. Roots tuberous. Europe.

EPIGÆA repens, R
(trailing arbutus)
COLOR: pink, white
HEIGHT: to 3 in.
BLOOM: April, May
SOIL: intense acid, peaty, sandy
SHADE: any excepting dense
REMARKS: do not transplant from wild. Evergreen leaves. Must have proper soil conditions. Fragrant. Difficult. Native.

EPIMEDIUM, several species, R
(barrenwort)
COLOR: pink, white, yellow, red, rose, purplish
HEIGHT: not above 1 ft.
BLOOM: spring
SOIL: rich, sandy preferred
SHADE: light under trees
REMARKS: very easy, small flowers, among rocks, ground cover spreading. Sometimes under trees, leaves remain almost all winter. Europe, Far East.

EUPATORIUM cœlestinum
(mist-flower, hardy ageratum)
COLOR: blue to violet
HEIGHT: to 3 ft.
BLOOM: September-October
SOIL: good garden
SHADE: half to light
REMARKS: useful in the border. Native.

EUPATORIUM rugosum
(white snakeroot)
COLOR: white
HEIGHT: to 4 ft.
BLOOM: August-October
SOIL: garden or woodland. Will grow in dry soil

SHADE: light to full
REMARKS: wild, or border planting but somewhat weedy. Native.

EUPHORBIA cyparissias
(cypress spurge)
COLOR: yellowish bracts
HEIGHT: to 1 ft.
BLOOM: July-August
SOIL: almost any
SHADE: half
REMARKS: a good ground cover, but rampageous. Eu. Eastern U.S.

FILIPENDULA hexapetala
(meadowsweet, dropwort)
COLOR: white
HEIGHT: 2-3 feet or more
BLOOM: early summer
SOIL: ordinary, even dry
SHADE: half
REMARKS: several species from 6 in. to 10 ft. high. Some have pink or white, single or double flowers. Fern-like foliage. Fragrant. Border, waterside, wild. Europe, Asia.

GALAX aphylla, R (galax)
COLOR: white
HEIGHT: flower spikes to 1 ½ ft.
BLOOM: July
SOIL: moist or dry, peaty
SHADE: any
REMARKS: spreading and happy

among rhododendrons. Stiff almost circular evergreen basal leaves bronze in autumn, good ground cover. Native.

GAULTHERIA procumbens, R
(wintergreen, checkerberry, teaberry)
COLOR: white
HEIGHT: to 5 in.
BLOOM: July, August
SOIL: sandy, peaty, acid
SHADE: any (light shade for bloom)
REMARKS: a shrublet, red berries in late summer. Attractive glossy ground cover in right environment. Native.

GENTIANA acaulis, R
(stemless gentian)
COLOR: dark blue
HEIGHT: to 4 in.
BLOOM: late spring
SOIL: rich, deep, moist, neutral
SHADE: half
REMARKS: the most popular kind in cultivation. Alps and Pyrenees.

GENTIANA andrewsii, R
(closed gentian)
COLOR: violet-blue or ultramarine, rarely white
HEIGHT: to 2 ft.

BLOOM: August, September
SOIL: good, deep humus, moist
SHADE: half
REMARKS: not difficult to grow.
Native.

GENTIANA crinita
(fringed gentian)

COLOR: violet-blue
HEIGHT: to 3 ft.
BLOOM: September
SOIL: damp, limy
SHADE: half
REMARKS: biennial, very difficult
to establish. Native.

GERANIUM maculatum, R
(wild or spotted cranesbill)

COLOR: rose-purple, rarely
white
HEIGHT: to 2 ft.
BLOOM: May-July
SOIL: moist preferred
SHADE: light
REMARKS: attractive in thin
woodland. Color better in shade.
Native.

GERANIUM pratense
(meadow cranesbill)

COLOR: purple, white form
HEIGHT: to 3 ft.
BLOOM: June, July
SOIL: good garden

SHADE: half to light
REMARKS: border plant, decorative foliage. Eurasia.

GOODYERA pubescens, R [Epipac-tis]
(downy rattlesnake plantain)

COLOR: white
HEIGHT: to 16 in.
BLOOM: July, August
SOIL: acid woodland
SHADE: any
REMARKS: white veined leaves,
nearly prostrate, wild garden.
Native.

HABENARIA blephariglottis, R
(white fringed orchis)

COLOR: white
HEIGHT: to 2 ft.
SOIL: boggy or moist, rich, acid
SHADE: half
REMARKS: one of our finest
natives.

HABENARIA ciliaris, R
(yellow fringed orchis)

COLOR: orange or yellow
HEIGHT: to 3 ½ ft.
BLOOM: July-August
SOIL: moist, rich
SHADE: light
REMARKS: striking species. Na-
tive.

HABENARIA psycodes grandiflora, R

(large purple fringed orchis)

COLOR: lilac

HEIGHT: to 3 ft.

BLOOM: mid July-August

SOIL: good, rich, moist, acid

SHADE: half to light

REMARKS: fragrant. Native.

HELLEBORUS niger altifolius, R

(Christmas-rose)

COLOR: white, or purplish-tinged

HEIGHT: to 1 ½ ft.

BLOOM: between Nov. and Mar.

SOIL: rich, well drained

SHADE: light, little sun

REMARKS: Plant where it can be seen from house or nearby. Evergreen leaves; do not disturb when once established. May need some protection. Europe.

HELLEBORUS orientalis, R

(lenten-rose)

COLOR: dark purple to greenish

HEIGHT: to 1 ft.

BLOOM: Lent, March to May

SOIL: rich, well drained

SHADE: half

REMARKS: may need some winter protection. Asia Minor.

HEMEROCALLIS species and named hybrids. (day-lilies)

COLOR: shades of red, pink, yellow, orange, apricot, bicolors

HEIGHT: to 5 ft.

BLOOM: May, June, July, August, September

SOIL: moist preferably

SHADE: strong light, half shade, filtered sun.

REMARKS: by careful selection of species, varieties and named hybrids, a long season of bloom may be arranged. Some are fragrant, some are dwarf, some evergreen. Far East. Some naturalized in U.S.

HEPATICA americana [H. triloba, Anemone H.], R

(liverleaf)

COLOR: lavender-blue, white or rose

HEIGHT: to 6 in.

BLOOM: early spring

SOIL: rich, well-drained loam

SHADE: among deciduous trees

REMARKS: they like sheltered banks but are not particular. New leaves appear after flowers. Evergreen. H. acutilobia is similar but with pointed instead of rounded leaves. Native.

HERACLEUM villosum [H. giganteum] (cow-parsnip)

COLOR: white
HEIGHT: to 10 ft.
BLOOM: July
SOIL: rich moist loam
SHADE: half
REMARKS: large plant, large leaves, subtropical effect. Rough places. Caucasus.

HESPERIS matronalis
(dames-rocket)

COLOR: white, lilac, purple
HEIGHT: 2-3 feet
BLOOM: June-July
SOIL: not particular, moist preferably
SHADE: half to light
REMARKS: fragrant, suggestive of phlox. Single and double varieties. Naturalizes well. Easily sown from seed. Europe.

HEUCHERA sanguinea and its varieties. (coral-bells)

COLOR: bright red, white, coral
HEIGHT: to 2 ft.
BLOOM: June-August
SOIL: good garden
SHADE: half
REMARKS: attractive and useful. Basal foliage. Good new forms. Native.

HOSTA [Funkia] many species and varieties. (plantain-lily)

COLOR: white, shades of lavender, blue
HEIGHT: 1 to 3 feet
BLOOM: July, August, September
SOIL: good garden, moist preferably
SHADE: any shade excepting deep
REMARKS: H. plantaginea has large white fragrant flowers. There are narrow leaf dwarf forms to those with large decorative foliage. Others with variegated green and white leaves, some green edged. Far East.

HOUSTONIA serpyllifolia, R
(creeping bluets)

COLOR: strong blue
HEIGHT: prostrate stems few inches long
BLOOM: spring
SOIL: moist preferably
SHADE: half
REMARKS: mats of tiny leaves. Native.

HYPOXIS hirsuta, R (star-grass)

COLOR: yellow
HEIGHT: 6-8 in.
BLOOM: June
SOIL: dry
SHADE: light

REMARKS: not showy but dainty, especially among rocks. Grass-like leaves. Native.

IBERIS sempervirens, R
(edging candytuft)

COLOR: white
HEIGHT: to 1 ft.
BLOOM: May
SOIL: good garden, well drained
SHADE: half (no more)
REMARKS: edging, border, rock or wall plant. Evergreen. Some good named varieties. Prune after flowering. S. Europe, W. Asia.

IRIS. See under bulbs.

JEFFERSONIA diphylla, R
(twin-leaf)

COLOR: white
HEIGHT: to 6-8 in.
BLOOM: May
SOIL: sandy, leafy, moist
SHADE: among deciduous trees
REMARKS: mass of starry bloom. Flowers somewhat like hepatica, basal leaves. Native.

LAMIUM maculatum and var. **al-bum** (dead nettle)

COLOR: white or rosy purple
HEIGHT: to 1½ ft., usually shorter
BLOOM: May-July

SOIL: any garden
SHADE: half
REMARKS: trailing with ascending stems. Useful as edging or among rocks. Europe, Asia. Naturalized in U.S.

LIGULARIA clivorum [Senecio c.]

COLOR: orange-yellow, dark brown disk
HEIGHT: to 4 ft.
BLOOM: August
SOIL: good garden
SHADE: light
REMARKS: daisy-like flowers. Japan, China.

LILIUM. See under Bulbs.

LINNÆA borealis, R (twin-flower)

COLOR: rose or white
HEIGHT: to 6 in.
BLOOM: June, July
SOIL: moist, peaty
SHADE: any
REMARKS: pendulous bells, trailing, evergreen leaves in dense mats, flowers on stalks. Must have right soil conditions. Native.

LOBELIA cardinalis
(cardinal-flower)

COLOR: red
HEIGHT: 3-4 ft.
BLOOM: July, August

SOIL: moist
SHADE: light to half
REMARKS: flowers on tall spikes, colonizes well near water. Native.

LOBELIA siphilitica
(large blue lobelia)

Similar to above but flowers are blue, blooming in August-September. Both plants self-sow.

LONICERA periclymenum, R
(woodbine)

COLOR: cream
HEIGHT: several feet, trailing
BLOOM: June-August
SOIL: good garden
SHADE: light
REMARKS: good ground cover. Red fruits. Fragrant, var. belgica and var. serotina are best for gardens. Europe, N. Africa, W. Asia.

LYSIMACHIA nummularia
(moneywort, creeping Jenny, creeping Charlie)

COLOR: yellow
HEIGHT: trailing
BLOOM: June-July
SOIL: any, even wet
SHADE: any
REMARKS: useful ground cover and attractive in difficult spots or

among stones. Europe, naturalized in America.

MAIANTHEMUM canadense, R
(Canada mayflower)

COLOR: white
HEIGHT: to 7 in., flowers in racemes
BLOOM: May-June
SOIL: well drained, cool, acid
SHADE: any
REMARKS: attractive, wild lily-of-the-valley. Small clusters of red berries, late summer. Foliage dies in summer. Native.

MALVA moschata
(musk mallow)

COLOR: rose or white
HEIGHT: to 2 ft.
BLOOM: summer
SOIL: any garden
SHADE: half
REMARKS: attractive border plant or wild garden, self sowing. Europe. Naturalized in N. America.

MAZUS reptans, R
COLOR: white or bluish, yellow center
HEIGHT: trailing
BLOOM: all summer
SOIL: dry

SHADE: half
REMARKS: useful between stones, mat forming. Himalayas, Australia.

MENTHA arvensis canadensis (wild mint)

COLOR: white or lilac-white
HEIGHT: to 2 ft.
BLOOM: July, August
SOIL: wet
SHADE: light
REMARKS: faint odor of mint, spreader. Native.

MENTHA piperita (peppermint)

COLOR: purplish
HEIGHT: to 3 ft.
BLOOM: July-August
SOIL: moist
SHADE: light
REMARKS: spreading by root stocks perhaps too aggressively. All mints are spreaders. Europe.

MENTHA requieni, R (Corsican mint)

COLOR: mauve
HEIGHT: creeper
BLOOM: July, August
SOIL: not too dry
SHADE: half
REMARKS: miniature creeper,

tiny flowers, low dense carpet between flagstones. Corsica.

MENTHA spicata (spearmint)

COLOR: pale purple
HEIGHT: to 2 ft.
BLOOM: July-August
SOIL: moist
SHADE: light
REMARKS: common garden species. Useful but rampageous. Europe. Naturalized in N. America.

MERTENSIA virginica, and other species, **R** (Virginia bluebell or cowslip)

COLOR: blue, pink when opening, white
HEIGHT: to 2 ft.
BLOOM: mid April to mid May
SOIL: rich, loamy, moist
SHADE: half, or anywhere among deciduous trees
REMARKS: ferns are often planted with it and occupy the space left vacant when the mertensia dies down. Native.

MIMULUS moschatus, R (musk-plant)

COLOR: yellow lightly dotted with brown
HEIGHT: creeping, usually to 6 in.

BLOOM: summer
SOIL: damp
SHADE: almost any
REMARKS: hardy trailer. Native.

MIMULUS ringens
(Allegheny monkey-flower)
COLOR: purple, blue, pink, white
HEIGHT: to 4 ft.
BLOOM: July, August
SOIL: wet
SHADE: light, among deciduous trees
REMARKS: flowers resemble snapdragon. Native.

MITCHELLA repens, R
(partridge-berry, twin-berry, squaw-berry)
COLOR: flesh to white
HEIGHT: trailing
BLOOM: June
SOIL: acid wood loam preferably
SHADE: any
REMARKS: attractive evergreen ground cover, red berries, tiny leaves. Native.

MITELLA diphylla, R
(bishops-cap)
COLOR: white
HEIGHT: to 1 ft.
BLOOM: April-May
SOIL: humus, moist

SHADE: half
REMARKS: flowers like tiny "caps." Dainty racemes. Native.

MONARDA didyma
(oswego-tea, bee-balm)
COLOR: scarlet, pink shades
HEIGHT: to 3 ft.
BLOOM: June-August
SOIL: moist woodland preferably, not particular
SHADE: light
REMARKS: effective and spreading, rather coarse, best at a distance. There are also salmon and white forms. M. fistulosa, (wild bergamot) has flowers lilac to purple in July. Also a hybrid form. Native.

MONOTROPA uniflora
(Indian-pipe, ghost flower)
COLOR: white to pinkish
HEIGHT: to 9 in.
BLOOM: July-August
SOIL: moist rich acid
SHADE: deep
REMARKS: woodland parasite, not in cultivation but a curiosity. Native.

MYOSOTIS scorpioides [M. palustris], R (forget-me-not)
COLOR: blue
HEIGHT: to 1 ½ ft.

BLOOM: May, June
SOIL: moist
SHADE: half to light
REMARKS: variety semperflorens
is a dwarf form to 8 in. high
blooming all summer. Europe,
Asia. Naturalized in America.

MYOSOTIS sylvatica, R
(forget-me-not)
COLOR: blue, varying to pink or
white
HEIGHT: to 2 feet
BLOOM: summer (var. alpestris
in spring)
SOIL: good garden
SHADE: half
REMARKS: treated as perennial,
though a self-sowing annual or
biennial. Europe, Asia.

NEPETA hederacea (ground-ivy,
gill-over-the- ground)
COLOR: light purple or light blue
HEIGHT: creeping
BLOOM: April-May
SOIL: any, but preferably moist
SHADE: light to full
REMARKS: perhaps too rapid
spreader but attractive ground
cover.

ŒNOTHERA fruticosa
(evening-primrose)
COLOR: sulphur yellow

HEIGHT: 1 to 3 ft.
BLOOM: June, July
SOIL: good garden
SHADE: half
REMARKS: easily grown. Var.
major and youngi are stocky and
floriferous. N. America.

OMPHALODES verna, R
(creeping forget-me-not)
COLOR: blue or white
HEIGHT: to 8 in.
BLOOM: April, May
SOIL: somewhat moist loam
SHADE: light
REMARKS: naturalizes easily.
Europe.

ORCHIS spectabilis, R
(showy orchis)
COLOR: sepals and petals purple,
lip white marked violet
HEIGHT: to 1 ft.
BLOOM: May-June
SOIL: moist, stony, cool
SHADE: any except dense
REMARKS: basal leaves, small
flower spikes. Fragrant, spread-
ing. Native.

**OXALIS montana [O. Americana],
R** (American wood-sorrel)
COLOR: pale pink or white,
purple veined
HEIGHT: to 3 in.

BLOOM: June
SOIL: deep cool acid wood
SHADE: any
REMARKS: leaves similar to shamrock. Native.

PACHYSANDRA procumbens
(Allegheny spurge)
COLOR: brownish white
HEIGHT: usually 6-8 in.
BLOOM: April-May
SOIL: woodland
SHADE: any
REMARKS: not evergreen. Slow spreading. Flowers in spikes from the base. Native.

PACHYSANDRA terminalis
(Japanese spurge)
COLOR: white
HEIGHT: under 12 in.
BLOOM: May
SOIL: rich preferably
SHADE: anywhere
REMARKS: evergreen ground cover, spreading. Easily grown by cuttings. Japan.

PETASITES fragrans
(winter-heliotrope, sweet coltsfoot)
COLOR: white, lilac, purple
HEIGHT: to 1 ft.
BLOOM: March to April
SOIL: any, even clay

SHADE: light
REMARKS: large leaves, vanillalike odor. Dense ground cover. Rough and wild-looking family. Good for rough places, semievergreen. Mediterranean region.

PETASITES japonicus
(giant butter-bur)
COLOR: greenish lemon
HEIGHT: to 6 ft.
BLOOM: March to April
SOIL: garden
SHADE: light
REMARKS: huge leaves 2-3 feet across. Sub-tropical effect. Island of Sakhalin.

PHLOX divaricata, R
(blue phlox, wild sweet-william)
COLOR: blue-lavender
HEIGHT: to 1½ ft.
BLOOM: May
SOIL: garden or woodland
SHADE: half or light shade of deciduous trees
REMARKS: colonizes beautifully in light woodland. Var. laphamii is recommended for the cultivated garden, as is 'Violet Queen.' Native.

PHLOX ovata
(mountain phlox)
COLOR: purple, sometimes pink

HEIGHT: to 15 in.
BLOOM: June, July
SOIL: fertile, well drained
SHADE: half
REMARKS: flowers in clusters. Native.

PHLOX paniculata
(summer perennial phlox)
COLOR: pink, white, salmon, scarlet, lilac, purple
HEIGHT: to 4 ft.
BLOOM: summer and early autumn
SOIL: rich
SHADE: half
REMARKS: in half shade this plant becomes somewhat coarser in appearance. Fragrant. Native.

PHLOX stolonifera [P. reptans], R
(creeping phlox)
COLOR: purple or violet
HEIGHT: to 10 inches
BLOOM: spring, early summer
SOIL: rich
SHADE: half
REMARKS: prostrate creeper. Native.

PHYSOSTEGIA virginiana
(false dragonhead)
COLOR: rose-pink or lilac, white
HEIGHT: to 4 ft.
BLOOM: July, August

SOIL: good garden
SHADE: light to half
REMARKS: snapdragon-like spikes. Var. vivid is deep pink and blooms August-September. All forms are spreading. Native.

PLATYCODON grandiflorum
(balloon-flower)
COLOR: deep blue, white
HEIGHT: to 2½ ft.
BLOOM: summer
SOIL: well drained, loamy
SHADE: half
REMARKS: attractive bell-shaped flowers. Several varieties. E. Asia.

PODOPHYLLUM peltatum
(may-apple)
COLOR: white
HEIGHT: to 1½ ft.
BLOOM: April, May
SOIL: rich moist
SHADE: of deciduous trees
REMARKS: yellow fruits in July. Large leaves make effective woodland carpet. Native.

POLEMONIUM cæruleum
(Jacobs-ladder, Greek valerian)
COLOR: blue, white
HEIGHT: 15 in. average
BLOOM: early summer
SOIL: rich, moisture preferred
SHADE: half

REMARKS: good border plant. Europe.

POLEMONIUM reptans, R
(Greek valerian)

COLOR: light blue
HEIGHT: to 1 ft.
BLOOM: May-July
SOIL: rich, loamy
SHADE: half
REMARKS: attractive in masses in border or rock garden. Sprawling. Native.

POLYGALA paucifolia, R
(fringed polygala, flowering winter-green)

COLOR: rose-purple, rarely white
HEIGHT: trailing 6-7 in.
BLOOM: May, June
SOIL: moist, rich, peaty
SHADE: any
REMARKS: must have right soil conditions. Native.

POLYGONATUM multiflorum
(Solomons-seal)

COLOR: greenish-cream
HEIGHT: to 3 ft.
BLOOM: May
SOIL: deep, rich, moist
SHADE: light to full
REMARKS: Europe and Asia, there is a tall native species to 6 ft.

P. commutatum (great solomons-seal).

PRIMULA auricula, R
(auricula primrose)

COLOR: many colors
HEIGHT: to 8 in.
BLOOM: April, May
SOIL: rich, good drainage
SHADE: half
REMARKS: leaves make fleshy rosette in a wall and are attractive the entire season. May need slight protection. Alps of Europe.

PRIMULA japonica, R
(Japanese primrose)

COLOR: purple, rose, white
HEIGHT: to 2 ft.
BLOOM: mid May-mid July
SOIL: rich moist
SHADE: light
REMARKS: lovely along light wooded walk. Border. Leaves stand up well through season. Good for streamside or lakeside. Japan.

PRIMULA polyantha, R
(polythanus primrose)

COLOR: white, yellow, copper, purple and others
HEIGHT: to 1 ft.
BLOOM: early spring
SOIL: rich moist

SHADE: half, or shade of deciduous trees

REMARKS: one of the earliest flowers to bloom. A hybrid group.

PRIMULA vulgaris, R [P. acaulis]
(common English primrose)

, COLOR: yellow, purple, blue
HEIGHT: to 6 in.
BLOOM: April, May
SOIL: rich moist, somewhat limy
SHADE: half, shade of deciduous trees; protect from hot sun.
REMARKS: one of the earliest spring flowers. Europe.

PULMONARIA angustifolia, R
(lungwort, cowslip)

COLOR: blue, violet
HEIGHT: to 10 in.
BLOOM: May
SOIL: cool, peaty
SHADE: light
REMARKS: easily cultivated. Border. Other species will also grow in shade, especially P. saccharata. Europe.

PYROLA elliptica, R
(shinleaf)

COLOR: white
HEIGHT: to 10 in.
BLOOM: June, July

SOIL: peaty, sandy woodland, not usual garden
SHADE: any, among evergreens
REMARKS: fragrant, waxy white flowers. P. asarifolia has pink flowers. Evergreen leaves, several species. Native.

RANUNCULUS aconitifolius
(fair-maids-of-France)

COLOR: white
HEIGHT: 2-3 ft.
SOIL: moist, well drained
SHADE: half
REMARKS: glossy leaves somewhat like monkshood. Var. floroplena has double flowers. Tuberous roots. Europe.

SAGINA subulata (pearlwort)

COLOR: white
HEIGHT: to 4 in.
BLOOM: July, August
SOIL: any garden
SHADE: light
REMARKS: densely tufted velvety evergreen carpet. Prefers level soil. *Warning:* This may become a lawn pest. Corsica.

SANGUINARIA canadensis, R
(bloodroot)

COLOR: white
HEIGHT: 6-8 in.
BLOOM: April

SOIL: rich woodland
SHADE: not too dense
REMARKS: attractive in masses among ferns. Var. multiplex beautiful, double flowers. Native.

SAPONARIA officinalis
(bouncing bet)

COLOR: pink or whitish
HEIGHT: to 3 ft.
BLOOM: June-August
SOIL: any garden
SHADE: light
REMARKS: easily grown. Too rapid spreader for mixed border. The double form is fragrant. W. Asia. Naturalized in N. Am.

SAXIFRAGA, virginiensis, R
(rock-foil)

COLOR: white
HEIGHT: 8-10 in.
BLOOM: April-June
SOIL: dry
SHADE: half to light
REMARKS: rosettes of leaves and flowers on spikes. Dry rock crevices. Many other species will stand partial shade. Native.

SEDUM acre, R (stonecrop)

COLOR: yellow
HEIGHT: creeping, flower stems 2-3 in. high
BLOOM: summer

SOIL: almost any garden
SHADE: light
REMARKS: the commonest sedum in cultivation. Creeping evergreen, forming mats. Form minus recommended. Europe.

SEDUM album, R

COLOR: white
HEIGHT: to 8 in.
BLOOM: July-August
SOIL: almost any garden
SHADE: half to light
REMARKS: evergreen creeper forming mats. Europe, Asia, N. Africa.

SEDUM kamtschaticum, R

COLOR: orange-yellow
HEIGHT: to 9 in.
BLOOM: July-August
SOIL: almost any garden
SHADE: half to light
REMARKS: compact ground cover. N.E. Asia.

SEDUM nevii, R

COLOR: white
HEIGHT: to 4 in.
BLOOM: June
SOIL: not particular
SHADE: light to full
REMARKS: rosettes of succulent leaves. Erect flower stems. Native.

SEDUM sarmentosum
COLOR: yellow
HEIGHT: prostrate
BLOOM: summer
SOIL: good garden
SHADE: light to half
REMARKS: evergreen Very
spreading. N. China, Japan.

SEDUM spurium, R
COLOR: pink to white
HEIGHT: to 9 in.
BLOOM: July
SOIL: almost any garden
SHADE: half to light
REMARKS: creeper forming mats.
Nearly evergreen, ground cover.
Caucasus.

SEDUM stoloniferum, R
COLOR: rose
HEIGHT: to 6 in.
BLOOM: July
SOIL: almost any garden
SHADE: half to light
REMARKS: creeping, nearly or
quite evergreen, ground cover.
S.W. Asia.

SEDUM ternatum, R
COLOR: white
HEIGHT: to 6 in.
BLOOM: May
SOIL: rich woodland for best
growth

SHADE: light to full
REMARKS: Evergreen. Native.

SENECIO clivorum. See Ligularia.

SENECIO tanguticus
COLOR: yellow
HEIGHT: to 7 ft., usually much
less
BLOOM: September and October
SOIL: good garden
SHADE: light
REMARKS: flowers in terminal
panicles. S. aureus is good for
damp places. W. China.

SHORTIA galacifolia, R
(oconee-bells)
COLOR: white
HEIGHT: to 8 in.
BLOOM: May
SOIL: humus, leaf mold, acid
wood loam
SHADE: among evergreens, full
REMARKS: shining evergreen
leaves, flowers solitary, nodding,
good ground cover. Native.

SMILACINA racemosa
(false solomons-seal)
COLOR: cream
HEIGHT: to 3 ft.
BLOOM: May-June
SOIL: well drained, rich, moist
SHADE: light

REMARKS: plumy flowers. Red berries. Native.

SOLIDAGO cæsia
(wreath golden-rod)
COLOR: yellow
HEIGHT: to 3 ft.
BLOOM: August-October
SOIL: grows weedy if soil is too rich
SHADE: light
REMARKS: neat and well behaved. The species flexicaulis is also recommended. Native.

SPIGELIA marilandica
(pink-root)
COLOR: red outside, yellow inside
HEIGHT: to 2 ft.
BLOOM: June-July
SOIL: good loam, moisture
SHADE: light, no intense sun
REMARKS: border. Flowers tubular. Native.

STACHYS lantana (lambs-ears)
COLOR: purple
HEIGHT: to 1½ ft.
BLOOM: June-July
SOIL: good garden
SHADE: half
REMARKS: border or edging. Silver-gray woolly leaves. Caucasus to Persia.

STELLARIA holostea (Easter bells)
COLOR: white
HEIGHT: to 2 ft.
BLOOM: May-June
SOIL: any garden
SHADE: any light
REMARKS: for covering dry banks where grass will not grow well, creeping rootstocks. Europe, N. Asia, escaped in eastern U.S.

STYLOPHORUM diphyllum, R
(celandine-poppy)
COLOR: yellow
HEIGHT: to 1½ ft.
BLOOM: April, May
SOIL: sandy, loamy
SHADE: light to half
REMARKS: grayish foliage, poppy-like flowers. Native.

THALICTRUM delavayi
(meadow-rue)
COLOR: purple or lilac
HEIGHT: to 3 ft.
BLOOM: July, August, but earlier than T. flavum
SOIL: well drained, loamy
SHADE: half to light
REMARKS: all are valued for graceful foliage. E. China.

THALICTRUM dioicum
(early meadow-rue)
COLOR: purplish-green

HEIGHT: to 2 ft.
BLOOM: early spring
SOIL: moist or dry woodland
SHADE: light
REMARKS: dainty and desirable.
Native.

THALICTRUM dipterocarpum
(meadow-rue)
COLOR: rose or lilac
HEIGHT: 2-6 ft.
BLOOM: July, August into September
SOIL: well drained, loamy
SHADE: half to light
REMARKS: persistent showy sepals. W. China.

THALICTRUM flavum
(meadow-rue)
COLOR: pale yellow
HEIGHT: to 4 ft.
BLOOM: July, August
SOIL: well drained, loamy
SHADE: half to light
REMARKS: dainty fern-like foliage. Europe.

TIARELLA cordifolia
(foam-flower)
COLOR: white
HEIGHT: to 1 ft.
BLOOM: May
SOIL: rich moist cool
SHADE: light

REMARKS: effective in masses in woodland or border. Native.

TOLMIEA menziesii
(pick-a-back plant)
COLOR: greenish sprays, not showy
BLOOM: spring
HEIGHT: less than two feet
SOIL: moist humus well drained
SHADE: full to light, very little sun
REMARKS: good foliage house plant. Basal leaves resemble those of Tiarella. Young plantlets are born at the base of each leaf blade, thus its common name. Winter hardy, good ground cover. Native.

TRADESCANTIA virginiana
(common spiderwort)
COLOR: violet-purple, rarely white, pink, blue
HEIGHT: to 3 ft.
BLOOM: nearly all summer
SOIL: moist preferably
SHADE: half
REMARKS: spreads by seed, leaves like coarse grass. Several improved hybrid forms. Native.

TRIENTALIS borealis, R
(star-flower)
COLOR: white

HEIGHT: to 9 in.
BLOOM: May
SOIL: damp cool humus
SHADE: light to full
REMARKS: dainty in wild garden.
Native.

TRILLIUM erectum, R
(wake-robin)
COLOR: brown-purple to green-
ish purple
HEIGHT: to 1 ft.
BLOOM: May
SOIL: rich moist
SHADE: any
REMARKS: naturalizes well under
trees. Native.

TRILLIUM grandiflorum, R
(large flowering trillium)
COLOR: white
HEIGHT: to 1 ½ ft.
BLOOM: May
SOIL: rich moist
SHADE: any
REMARKS: very handsome.
Native.

TRILLIUM undulatum, R
(painted trillium)
COLOR: white, veined purple at
base of petals
HEIGHT: to 2 ft.
BLOOM: May-June
SOIL: very acid woodland

SHADE: any
REMARKS: all the Trillium species
will grow in shade. T. stylosum,
T. sessile, T. discolor and T. simile
are especially desirable. Native.

TROLLIUS europæus
(globe-flower)
COLOR: lemon yellow
HEIGHT: to 2 ft.
BLOOM: May-June
SOIL: deep moist, rich
SHADE: half
REMARKS: showy flowers. Easy
to grow. Europe.

TULIP. See under Bulbs.

UVULARIA, all species
(bellwort, wild oats)
COLOR: yellow
HEIGHT: 1-1 ½ ft.
BLOOM: May, June
SOIL: rich, peaty
SHADE: any but dense
REMARKS: gawky plant with small
bell-shaped flowers, will thrive
on north side of wall. Good with
ferns. Native.

VALERIANA officinalis
(common valerian, garden helio-
trope)
COLOR: pale pink, lavender,
white

HEIGHT: 2-4 feet
BLOOM: summer
SOIL: moist
SHADE: light
REMARKS: fragrant. Deciduous woodland, waterside, bog garden, spreading. Europe, Asia, nat. U.S.

VANCOUVERIA hexandra, R
(American barrenwort)
COLOR: white
HEIGHT: to 1 ½ ft.
BLOOM: May, June
SOIL: rich, leaf mold
SHADE: light to full
REMARKS: at home in coniferous woods, as in the border. All species will grow in shade. V. chrysantha is most choice in less shade. Native.

VERONICA filiformis
COLOR: blue
HEIGHT: few inches
BLOOM: April, May
SOIL: damp preferably
SHADE: half
REMARKS: may behave as an annual. Excellent ground cover. Sometimes seen invading a lawn. Lovely in flower. Asia Minor.

VERONICA officinalis
(common speedwell)
COLOR: pale blue

HEIGHT: prostrate, flower spikes to 3 in.
BLOOM: May-July
SOIL: almost any
SHADE: any
REMARKS: ground cover under trees. Spreader, somewhat coarse Europe, Asia, N. America.

VERONICA repens, R
(creeping veronica)
COLOR: rose or bluish, lavender
HEIGHT: creeping
BLOOM: May-July
SOIL: preferably moist, sandy
SHADE: half
REMARKS: moss-like, good among stones, ground cover among bulbs. Corsica.

VINCA minor
(periwinkle, running myrtle)
COLOR: lilac-blue (white, purple and rose forms)
HEIGHT: trailing, 1 ft.
BLOOM: May
SOIL: common garden
SHADE: any
REMARKS: carpets bare spaces anywhere. Evergreen. Bowles var. is recommended and others including 'Miss Jekyll,' a white bloom. Europe, runs wild in E. U.S.

VIOLA blanda, R
(sweet white violet)
COLOR: white
BLOOM: April, May
SOIL: preferably moist
SHADE: light to full
REMARKS: grows under evergreens, narrow reflexed petals. Native.

VIOLA canadensis, R (Canada violet)
COLOR: white inside, yellow base, outside tinged violet
HEIGHT: to 1 ft.
BLOOM: May-July
SOIL: fairly rich
SHADE: full
REMARKS: pointed heart-shaped leaves. Native.

VIOLA odorata, R
(sweet garden or florists violet)
COLOR: deep violet
HEIGHT: stemless, making runners
BLOOM: April-May
SOIL: rich
SHADE: light to half
REMARKS: fragrant. Many fine named varieties. Europe, Africa, Asia.

VIOLA pallens, R
COLOR: white
BLOOM: April-May

SOIL: rich moist
SHADE: light
REMARKS: often confused with V. blanda. Native.

VIOLA palmata, R (palmate violet)
COLOR: violet, purple
HEIGHT: 2-6 in.
BLOOM: April, May
SOIL: moist, or fairly dry
SHADE: light
REMARKS: native.

VIOLA papilionacea, R
(common blue violet)
COLOR: light or deep violet
HEIGHT: to 6 in.
BLOOM: April-June
SOIL: preferably moist
SHADE: light to full
REMARKS: spreads rapidly. Native.

VIOLA pubescens, R
COLOR: bright yellow
HEIGHT: to 1 ft.
BLOOM: April-May
SOIL: rich
SHADE: light to full
REMARKS: will grow under evergreens. Native.

VIOLA rotundifolia, R
(round-leaved violet)
COLOR: yellow
HEIGHT: to 4 in.

BLOOM: April, May
SOIL: preferably moist
SHADE: cool, full, under ever-
greens
REMARKS: good ground cover.
Native. Earliest to bloom.

VIOLA septentrionalis var. alba, R
(large white violet)
COLOR: white
HEIGHT: to 6 in.
BLOOM: April-May
SOIL: good garden
SHADE: any but dense
REMARKS: one of the handsomest
violets, though its exact identity
is a mystery.

VIOLA striata, R
COLOR: cream

HEIGHT: to 2 ft.
BLOOM: May-June
SOIL: rich
SHADE: light to half
REMARKS: spreads rapidly.
Native.

VIOLA tricolor, R
(Johnny-jump-up, heart's ease,
wild pansy)
COLOR: purple, blue, yellow,
white
HEIGHT: 8 in.
BLOOM: best spring and fall
SOIL: rich, moist
SHADE: half
REMARKS: self-sowing annual, for
better bloom keep well pruned.
Europe origin.

DECIDUOUS SHRUBS AND TREES FOR
VARYING DEGREES OF SHADE

ACANTHOPANAX sieboldianum
(five-leaved aralia)

COLOR: greenish white
HEIGHT: average 6 ft.
SOIL: good garden
SHADE: light to full
REMARKS: valuable for its foliage
which resembles miniature Vir-
ginia creeper leaves. Other

species also grow in shade. Japan.

ACER palmatum and varieties
(Japanese maple)
HEIGHT: to 20 ft.
SOIL: good garden
SHADE: light
REMARKS: graceful leaves, beau-
tiful color, green, red-purple,
orange. Japan.

ACER pennsylvanicum
(moosewood)

HEIGHT: under 40 feet
SOIL: ordinary
SHADE: light
REMARKS: small tree, large light green leaves, clear yellow in fall. Twigs and branchlets are greenish striped white. Rather coarse for lawn use. Native.

ACER spicatum (mountain maple)

HEIGHT: under 30 ft.
COLOR: white spikes
BLOOM: spring
SOIL: ordinary
SHADE: light
REMARKS: large shrub or small tree. Leaves orange-scarlet in fall. Winged samaris bright red in summer. Eastern N. Am.

AMELANCHIER canadensis
(service-berry, juneberry, shadbush, downy shadblow)

COLOR: white
HEIGHT: to 30 ft.
BLOOM: April, May
SOIL: good garden
SHADE: half
REMARKS: red berries (attractive to birds) turn almost black in June. Flowers before leaves. Native.

ARONIA arbutifolia
(red choke-berry)

COLOR: white or tinged red
HEIGHT: to 10 ft.
BLOOM: April, May
SOIL: good garden, moist or dry
SHADE: light
REMARKS: red berries in autumn and winter. Attractive to birds. Other species have deep purple or black fruits. Native.

AZALEA
Botanically, azaleas are classed in the genus Rhododendron (which see under Evergreen Shrubs, page 217). There are many handsome hybrid forms in choice colorings particularly the deciduous azaleas, for example the rustica and pontica hybrids. Given peaty acid soil they usually bloom at their best in filtered sunlight and shadow, light or half shade. Following is a group of azalea species mostly native but some from the Far East.

AZALEA arborescens [Rhododendron a.] (sweet azalea)

COLOR: white or pinkish
HEIGHT: to 10 ft.
BLOOM: June-July
SOIL: loose acid humus

SHADE: light to half
REMARKS: fragrant. Native.

AZALEA calendulacea [Rho. calendulaceum] (flame azalea)

COLOR: orange-yellow to scarlet, lemon, buff
HEIGHT: to 10 ft.
BLOOM: May-June
SOIL: peaty acid
SHADE: light
REMARKS: native.

AZALEA mucronulata [Rho. mucronulatum]

COLOR: pale rosy purple
HEIGHT: to 6 ft.
BLOOM: March-April
SOIL: peaty acid
SHADE: half
REMARKS: N. China.

AZALEA japonica [Rho. japonicum]

COLOR: orange-red to scarlet
HEIGHT: to 6 ft.
BLOOM: April-May
SOIL: peaty acid
SHADE: half
REMARKS: Japan.

AZALEA obtusa kaempferi [Rho. obtusum kaempferi]

COLOR: red to pink
HEIGHT: to 12 ft.
BLOOM: May

SOIL: peaty acid
SHADE: half
REMARKS: this may be evergreen in some localities. The kurume and hinodegeri azaleas are products of this species and both are evergreen. Japan.

AZALEA mollis [Rho. molle]

COLOR: golden yellow
HEIGHT: to 5 ft.
BLOOM: April, May
SOIL: peaty acid
SHADE: half
REMARKS: may need protection; very lovely color. China.

AZALEA nudiflora [Rho. nudiflorum] (pinxter-flower)

COLOR: pale pink or white
HEIGHT: to 6 ft. or more
BLOOM: April, May
SOIL: good acid
SHADE: light
REMARKS: native.

AZALEA rosea [Rho. roseum] (downy pinxterbloom)

COLOR: pink
HEIGHT: to 12 ft.
BLOOM: May
SOIL: peaty acid, but any good soil will do
SHADE: light
REMARKS: sometimes considered

a var. of R. nudiflorum. Fragrant. Native.

AZALEA schlippenbachii [Rho. s.]
(royal azalea)
COLOR: pink spotted brown
HEIGHT: to 15 ft.
BLOOM: May
SOIL: peaty acid
SHADE: half
REMARKS: fragrant. Far East.

AZALEA vaseyi [Rho. v.]
(pink-shell azalea)
COLOR: pink spotted with brown
HEIGHT: to 15 ft.
BLOOM: May
SOIL: loose acid humus, moist
SHADE: light
REMARKS: attractive autumn foliage. Native.

AZALEA viscosa [Rho. viscosum]
(white swamp honeysuckle)
COLOR: white, or pink (rarely)
HEIGHT: to 10 ft.
BLOOM: June-July
SOIL: acid humus
SHADE: light
REMARKS: fragrant. Native.

CALYCANTHUS floridus
(Carolina allspice, sweet-shrub)
COLOR: brownish or dark reddish purple
HEIGHT: to 10 ft.
BLOOM: spring
SOIL: well drained rich
SHADE: light
REMARKS: fragrant flowers, foliage and twigs, aromatic when crushed. Native.

CERCIS canadensis
(Judas-tree, redbud)
COLOR: rosy purple buds and deep pink flowers
HEIGHT: to 40 ft.
BLOOM: April, May
SOIL: loamy, sandy
SHADE: half
REMARKS: buds before leaves. Tree or tree-like shrub, pea-like flowers. Native.

CHÆNOMELES lagenaria [Cydonia japonica] (Japanese quince)
COLOR: scarlet, pink, orange, white
HEIGHT: to 10 ft.
BLOOM: March-April
SOIL: good garden
SHADE: half
REMARKS: greenish yellow fruits. A dwarf species is C. japonica. China.

CLETHRA alnifolia
(summer sweet, sweet pepperbush)
COLOR: white spikes

HEIGHT: to 10 ft.
BLOOM: July
SOIL: moist
SHADE: any except dense
REMARKS: fragrant, good rear border plant. C. acuminata is also fine. Native.

CORNUS alba
(tartarian dogwood)

COLOR: whitish or tinted blue
HEIGHT: to 10 ft.
BLOOM: June
SOIL: moist
SHADE: light
REMARKS: blood red twigs, white berries late summer. Var. sibirica has bright coral branches. Siberia, North China.

CORNUS alternifolia
(pagoda dogwood)

COLOR: white
HEIGHT: to 25 ft.
BLOOM: June
SOIL: good garden or woodland
SHADE: light
REMARKS: horizontal spreading branches, dark blue fruits summer and autumn. Native.

CORNUS amomum
(silky dogwood)

COLOR: white
HEIGHT: to 10 ft.

BLOOM: June, July
SOIL: good garden or woodland
SHADE: light
REMARKS: pale blue fruits, and purple branches. Thicket former. Native.

CORNUS canadensis is under Perennials.

CORNUS florida
(flowering dogwood)

COLOR: white
HEIGHT: to 40 ft.
BLOOM: May
SOIL: good garden or woodland
SHADE: light
REMARKS: red fruits in autumn. Practically all dogwoods are attractive to birds. Var. rubra has pink or rose bracts. Native.

CORNUS mas
(cornelian-cherry)

COLOR: yellow, small, before leaves
HEIGHT: to 20 ft.
BLOOM: April
SOIL: good garden
SHADE: light
REMARKS: compact heavy foliage, good screen. Red cherry-like fruits in late summer. S. Europe. Orient.

CORNUS racemosa (gray dogwood)

COLOR: white

HEIGHT: to 15 ft.

BLOOM: June

SOIL: normal, will stand dry soil

SHADE: light to half

REMARKS: white fruits on pink stems all winter. Purple autumn colors. Thicket former. Native.

CORNUS rugosa

COLOR: white

HEIGHT: to 15 ft.

BLOOM: May-June

SOIL: loamy

SHADE: light

REMARKS: attractive large round leaves. Fruit light blue. Native.

CORNUS stolonifera

(red-osier dogwood)

COLOR: white

HEIGHT: to 10 ft.

BLOOM: May

SOIL: moist

SHADE: light

REMARKS: fruits bluish white in late summer. Dark blood-red branches, a thicket former. Var. flaviramea has yellow twigs. Native.

CRATAEGUS crus-galli (cockspur thorn, thornapple, hawthorn)

COLOR: white

HEIGHT: to 25 ft.

BLOOM: May, June

SOIL: loamy

SHADE: half

REMARKS: fruits like tiny apples, bright red. Leaves orange and scarlet in fall. Native.

DAPHNE mezereum

(February daphne)

COLOR: lilac-purple

HEIGHT: to 4 ft.

BLOOM: February-April

SOIL: sandy compost of peat and loam, well drained

SHADE: half

REMARKS: fragrant, bloom before leaves, scarlet fruit. Europe, West Asia.

DIERVILLA sessilifolia

(southern bush-honeysuckle)

COLOR: deep yellow trumpet

HEIGHT: 4½ ft.

BLOOM: June

SOIL: good garden

SHADE: half to light

REMARKS: rough ground cover, spreading, rocky hillsides, banks, soil binder. D. lonicera (dwarf bush-honeysuckle) is similar. Native.

ENKIANTHUS campanulatus

(redvein enkianthus)

COLOR: yellow or pale orange veined red
HEIGHT: to 30 ft.
BLOOM: May
SOIL: peaty, sandy, well drained, acid
SHADE: light
REMARKS: foliage brilliant red in autumn. Flowers bell-shaped. White-flowered E. perulatus is lower growing. Japan.

EUONYMUS alatus
(winged euonymus)
COLOR: yellowish
HEIGHT: to 8 ft.
BLOOM: May-June
SOIL: good garden
SHADE: half
REMARKS: foliage handsome in autumn. Fruits have purplish caps, brown seeds with orange aril. China and Japan.

EUONYMUS americanus
(strawberry-bush)
COLOR: yellowish or reddish green
HEIGHT: to 8 ft.
BLOOM: June
SOIL: good garden
SHADE: half
REMARKS: autumn-colored leaves, crimson, bur-like fruits in September. Native.

EUONYMUS atropurpureus
(wahoo, burning-bush)
COLOR: purple
HEIGHT: to 25 ft.
BLOOM: June
SOIL: good garden
SHADE: half
REMARKS: pink and vermilion fruit in October. Native.

EUONYMUS obovatus
(running strawberry bush)
COLOR: red autumn foliage, pink berries
SOIL: moist, some lime preferred
SHADE: half to light
REMARKS: Used primarily as ground cover. Quick growing.

EUONYMUS. See also under Evergreens.

FORSYTHIA suspensa
(golden-bells)
COLOR: golden yellow
HEIGHT: to 10 ft.
BLOOM: April, May
SOIL: good garden
SHADE: spring sun, summer half shade
REMARKS: graceful, with drooping branches. China.

FOTHERGILLA species

COLOR: white, in spikes
HEIGHT: 3-9 ft.
BLOOM: May
SOIL: moist, rich, sandy, peaty
SHADE: half
REMARKS: bright yellow and scarlet autumn foliage. There are dwarf, intermediate and tall species. Effective in front of evergreens. Native.

HAMAMELIS mollis
(Chinese witch-hazel)

COLOR: golden yellow
HEIGHT: to 30 ft.
BLOOM: March or earlier
SOIL: good garden, moist
SHADE: light
REMARKS: blooms before spring, fragrant. The Japanese species, H. japonica, is also recommended. China.

HAMAMELIS vernalis
(vernal witch-hazel)

COLOR: pinkish orange
HEIGHT: to 6 ft.
BLOOM: between January and March
SOIL: good garden
SHADE: light
REMARKS: blooms in winter. Fragrant. Native.

HAMAMELIS virginiana
(common witch-hazel)

COLOR: yellow
HEIGHT: to 15 ft.
BLOOM: between September and November
SOIL: will stand dry soil
SHADE: light
REMARKS: yellow leaves in fall, sometimes last flower to bloom. Native.

HALESIA carolina
(silverbell, snowdrop tree)

COLOR: white
HEIGHT: 20-40 ft.
BLOOM: May
SOIL: loamy, well drained
SHADE: light
REMARKS: interesting four-winged fruits. Clear yellow autumn color. Rapid growing often shrub-like and spreading. Native.

HYDRANGEA arborescens
(smooth hydrangea)

COLOR: white
HEIGHT: to 10 ft.
BLOOM: July
SOIL: rich, preferably somewhat moist
SHADE: half
REMARKS: variety grandiflora

(Snowhill H.) is excellent for the cultivated garden, and has large heads of flowers. Cut stems to ground in autumn. Many species will grow in half shade, notably H. quercifolia. Native.

HYDRANGEA. See also under Vines.

HYPERICUM calycinum
(St. Johnswort, Aaron's beard)
COLOR: yellow
HEIGHT: to 1 ft.
BLOOM: July-August
SOIL: sandy
REMARKS: sometimes evergreen, or half evergreen ground cover, spreading. Europe, Asia Minor.

HYPERICUM prolificum
(shrubby St. Johnswort)
COLOR: yellow
HEIGHT: 3-5 ft.
BLOOM: July
SOIL: good garden
SHADE: light
REMARKS: shrubby, mounded, floriferous. The species H. frondosum (golden St. Johnswort) has larger flowers, 2 in. across. Native.

ILEX verticillata
(black alder, winterberry)

COLOR: whitish
HEIGHT: to 10 ft.
BLOOM: June-July
SOIL: moist
SHADE: half
REMARKS: bright red fruits in October, remaining until winter. Not interesting to birds. Native.

ILEX. See also under Evergreen Shrubs.

KERRIA japonica
(Japanese kerria)
COLOR: yellow
HEIGHT: to 8 ft.
BLOOM: April, May
SOIL: ordinary, well drained
SHADE: light to half
REMARKS: green stems attractive in winter. Var. pleniflora has double flowers and is best. China.

LEYCESTERIA formosa
(Formosa honeysuckle)
COLOR: lavender to white, small, purple bracts
HEIGHT: 6 ft.
BLOOM: late summer
SOIL: good garden
SHADE: light
REMARKS: red-purple berries, attractive to birds. Hardy to

southern New England if protected. Formosa.

LIGUSTRUM amurense
(amur privet)
COLOR: cream white
HEIGHT: to 15 ft.
BLOOM: June, July
SOIL: good garden
SHADE: light
REMARKS: good, hardy hedge plant, half evergreen. Blue-black berries. Will stand city conditions. China.

LIGUSTRUM obtusifolium, var. **regelianum [L. Ibota]**
(regels privet)
COLOR: cream white
HEIGHT: to 10 ft.
BLOOM: June
SOIL: good garden
SHADE: light
REMARKS: flowers in lateral clusters, blue-black berries autumn and winter. Best of all deciduous privets. Will stand city conditions better than any of the privets. Japan.

LIGUSTRUM ovalifolium
(California privet)
COLOR: cream white
HEIGHT: to 15 ft.
BLOOM: July

SOIL: good garden
SHADE: light
REMARKS: handsome, stiff habit, fine hedge. Grows well by the sea. Almost evergreen. Berries black (if any). Will stand city conditions. Japan.

LIGUSTRUM vulgare
(common privet)
COLOR: cream white
HEIGHT: to 15 ft.
BLOOM: June, July
SOIL: good garden
SHADE: light
REMARKS: black shining berries, semi-evergreen, will stand city conditions. Mediterranean region, naturalized in eastern U.S.

LINDERA benzoin (spice-bush)
COLOR: greenish yellow
HEIGHT: to 15 ft.
BLOOM: April
SOIL: moist
SHADE: light
REMARKS: red berries attractive to birds. Yellow autumn leaves. Native.

LONICERA fragrantissima
(winter honeysuckle)
COLOR: cream white
HEIGHT: to 8 ft.
BLOOM: March, April

SOIL: good garden
SHADE: half
REMARKS: red berries, half evergreen, early sweet-scented flowers. China.

LONICERA maackii
(amur honeysuckle)

COLOR: white to yellowish
HEIGHT: to 15 ft.
BLOOM: May
SOIL: good garden
SHADE: half
REMARKS: foliage remains until
late autumn, esp. on Var. podo-
carpa. Red berries. Var. erube-
scens has pink flowers larger
than the above. China.

LONICERA morrowi
(morrow honeysuckle)

COLOR: white or yellowish
HEIGHT: to 8 ft.
BLOOM: May-June
SOIL: good garden
SHADE: light
REMARKS: dark red berries,
mound-like habit. Japan.

LONICERA tatarica
(tatarian honeysuckle)

COLOR: white to pink
HEIGHT: to 10 ft.
BLOOM: May-June
SOIL: good garden

SHADE: light
REMARKS: red berries in July.
Useful and hardy. Several good
varieties. Russia to Turkestan.

LYONIA mariana (stagger-bush)

COLOR: white
HEIGHT: to 6 ft.
BLOOM: May-June
SOIL: acid, peaty, or boggy
SHADE: light to half
REMARKS: attractive autumn col-
orings. Native.

MAGNOLIA virginiana [M. glauca]
(sweet bay)

COLOR: white
HEIGHT: to 60 feet
BLOOM: June-July
SOIL: good garden, moist
SHADE: half
REMARKS: bushy in northerly
locality, tree-like in the South.
Fragrant. Native.

PHILADELPHUS coronarius
(mock-orange)

COLOR: creamy
HEIGHT: to 10 ft.
BLOOM: June
SOIL: good garden
SHADE: half, open situation
REMARKS: fragrant. Will stand
city conditions. Europe, S.W.
Asia.

RHAMNUS cathartica
(buckthorn)

HEIGHT: to 12 ft.
SOIL: poor, sandy, clay
SHADE: light
REMARKS: vigorous, protective hedge. Small berries green to red to black, liked by birds. Europe, Asia, Africa. Nat. in E. U.S.

RHODOTYPOS tetrapetala [R. kerrioides] (jetbead)

COLOR: white
HEIGHT: to 7 ft.
BLOOM: May-June
SOIL: good garden
SHADE: light
REMARKS: shiny black berries, bright green foliage. Japan.

ROBINIA hispida (rose acacia)

COLOR: rose or pale purple
HEIGHT: to 7 ft.
BLOOM: May, June
SOIL: any, even sandy and dry
SHADE: light
REMARKS: spreads rampantly by suckers, thrifty. Rough ground cover needs space. Native.

ROSA

Most roses will bloom in part day shade. The wild or vigorous climbers may stand even more.

RUBUS odoratus
(flowering raspberry)

COLOR: rose purple
HEIGHT: to 6 ft.
BLOOM: July
SOIL: moist
SHADE: light
REMARKS: prefers rich shady woods and banks. Red raspberries not palatable to man or bird. Large flowers but coarse shrub. Native.

SASSAFRAS albidum

COLOR: yellow
HEIGHT: to 60 ft.
BLOOM: April, May
SOIL: garden or woodland
SHADE: light to half
REMARKS: tree or shrub, fruits dark blue, red stalks. Mitten-shaped leaves turn red, yellow-orange. Native.

STAPHYLEA colchica, others
(bladdernut)

COLOR: white, clusters
HEIGHT: 12-15 ft.
BLOOM: May
SOIL: moïst, rich
SHADE: half
REMARKS: wide spreading, curious brown inflated seed pods. Caucasus.

STYRAX japonica
(Japanese snowbell)
COLOR: white
HEIGHT: to 30 ft.
BLOOM: June, July
SOIL: light porous
SHADE: light
REMARKS: handsome tree or shrub in bloom, symmetrical. Border or specimen. Japan, China.

SYMPHORICARPOS albus [S. racemosus] var. **lævigatus**
(snowberry, waxberry)
COLOR: pinkish, bell shaped
HEIGHT: to 6 ft.
BLOOM: July
SOIL: good garden
SHADE: half
REMARKS: thicket former, white berries in autumn. Native.

SYMPLOCOS paniculata
(Asiatic sweetleaf)
COLOR: white, small white clusters
HEIGHT: to 35 ft.
BLOOM: May
SOIL: not demanding
SHADE: half
REMARKS: fragrant. Pale bright blue berries in October, liked by birds. Too wide spreading for small garden. Far East.

VACCINIUM angustifolium var. **laevifolium**
(lowbush blueberry)
COLOR: small greenish white
HEIGHT: to 2 ft.
BLOOM: April, May
SOIL: peaty acid
SHADE: light to full
REMARKS: woodland ground cover. Red autumn color. Food for birds. Other blueberries such as V. corymbosum, stamineum and vacillans will grow in shade. Native.

VIBURNUM acerifolium
(dockmackie, maple-leaved viburnum)
COLOR: white
HEIGHT: to 6 ft.
BLOOM: May-June
SOIL: normal
SHADE: light to full
REMARKS: used primarily for dark purple to pale rose autumn coloring. Fruits purple-black in autumn, attractive to birds. Thrives in shade. Native.

VIBURNUM alnifolium
(hobble-bush, American wayfaring tree)
COLOR: white
HEIGHT: to 10 ft.
BLOOM: May-June

SOIL: garden or woodland
SHADE: light
REMARKS: thrives in shade. Berries first red, then dark purple. Large foliage deep red in autumn. Native.

VIBURNUM cassinoides
(withe-rod)

COLOR: cream white
HEIGHT: to 12 ft.
BLOOM: June-July
SOIL: normal, will stand wet conditions
SHADE: light to half
REMARKS: fruits from yellow-green to pink to blue-black. Native.

VIBURNUM opulus
(European cranberry-bush)

COLOR: white
HEIGHT: to 12 ft.
BLOOM: May-June
SOIL: good garden
SHADE: light to half
REMARKS: red berries, fall and winter. Europe, N. Africa, N. Asia.

VIBURNUM prunifolium
(black-haw)

COLOR: white
HEIGHT: to 15 ft.
BLOOM: May

SOIL: loamy
SHADE: light
REMARKS: blue-black berries late summer. Horizontal branching, good specimen. Native.

VIBURNUM sieboldii

COLOR: cream white
HEIGHT: to 10 ft. or more
BLOOM: May, June
SOIL: any good
SHADE: half
REMARKS: red autumn foliage. Berries pink to red to black. Handsome. Japan.

WEIGELA florida

COLOR: rose
HEIGHT: to 8 and 10 ft.
BLOOM: May
SOIL: good garden
SHADE: light
REMARKS: will stand city conditions. Often included in the genus Diervilla, but distinct. N. China, Korea.

XANTHORHIZA simplicissima
(shrub yellow-root)

COLOR: brownish purple
HEIGHT: to 2 ft.
BLOOM: April
SOIL: any good, damp preferred
SHADE: light to full
REMARKS: rapid spreader, good

ground cover, yellow roots. Yellow autumn coloring. Native.

ZENOBIA pulverulenta
(dusty zenobia)
COLOR: white
HEIGHT: to 6 ft.

BLOOM: May, June
SOIL: sandy acid
SHADE: half to light
REMARKS: gray-green foliage. Interesting contrast when grown with other acid-loving plants. Native.

EVERGREEN SHRUBS AND TREES FOR VARYING DEGREES OF SHADE

ARCTOSTAPHYLOS uva-ursi
(bearberry)
COLOR: white or pinkish
HEIGHT: trailing
SOIL: sandy, porous, acid
BLOOM: late April
SHADE: half (no more)
REMARKS: attractive ground cover for sandy or rocky slopes, red berries. Sometimes difficult to establish. Europe, N. Asia, N. America.

AZALEA. See also under Rhododendron (evergreen) and under Azalea (deciduous).

AZALEA amœna [Rhododendron obtusum amœnum]
COLOR: red-purple
HEIGHT: to 3 ft. or more
BLOOM: April-May
SOIL: porous, acid
SHADE: any except deep

REMARKS: very hardy, small glossy foliage, color difficult. Japan.

AZALEA hinodegiri [Rho. obtusum japonicum]
COLOR: red
HEIGHT: to 3 ft.
BLOOM: April, May
SOIL: porous, acid
SHADE: light
REMARKS: does not bloom profusely in shade. Japan.

AZALEA mucronata [Rho. mucronatum, also R. ledifolium and var. album]
COLOR: white
HEIGHT: to 6 ft.
BLOOM: May
SOIL: porous, acid
SHADE: light to half
REMARKS: large fragrant flowers, foliage less attractive than

amœna and hinodegiri. This species is sometimes called 'Indica Alba.' China.

BERBERIS julianæ
(wintergreen barberry)
COLOR: yellow
HEIGHT: to 6 ft.
BLOOM: May
SOIL: well-drained light loam
SHADE: half
REMARKS: may not berry in shade. Color blue-black. China.

BUXUS microphylla japonica
(Japanese box)
HEIGHT: to 6 ft.
SOIL: good garden
SHADE: half to light
REMARKS: somewhat more hardy than the common box. Japan.

BUXUS sempervirens
(common box)
HEIGHT: to 25 ft.
SOIL: good well-drained
SHADE: light to half
REMARKS: not reliably hardy above Southern New England, suffruticosa is a dwarf form with small leaves. Europe, N. Africa, W. Asia.

CHAMAECYPARIS obtusa, dwarf forms
(hinoki cypress)
HEIGHT: 3 inches to a few feet

SOIL: rich garden
SHADE: half
REMARKS: other species will also grow in shade. The obtusa dwarfs such as variety compacta, pigmea and others are rock garden or ground cover plants. Japan.

CHAMAEDAPHNE calyculata
(leatherleaf)
COLOR: white, nodding
HEIGHT: 1-5 ft.
BLOOM: April, May
SOIL: peaty, moist, even wet
SHADE: half
REMARKS: evergreen. Var. nana good for rock garden where there is moisture. Europe, Asia, N. America.

COTONEASTER salicifolia floccosa
(willow-leaved cotoneaster)
COLOR: white
HEIGHT: to 15 ft.
BLOOM: June
SOIL: good garden soil
SHADE: half
REMARKS: semi-evergreen, red orange berries autumn and winter. Willow-like foliage. China.

DAPHNE cneorum, R
(garland flower)
COLOR: pink

HEIGHT: to 18 in.
BLOOM: April, May
SOIL: loose, loamy, sandy, well drained
SHADE: half (no more)
REMARKS: attractive among rocks. Tiny leaves, very desirable, fragrant. Mountains of Europe.

EUONYMUS fortunei and varieties
HEIGHT: shrubs to 4-5 ft., or vines
SOIL: good garden
SHADE: full to light
REMARKS: var. carrierei and var. vegetus have berries like bittersweet. Both are shrubs but vegetus climbs as well. Var. coloratus is a ground cover with leaves turning purplish in fall. Several small leaf var. are excellent climbers by rootlike holdfasts but no berries. They are vars. radicans, and two smaller leaf forms minimus and kewensis. China.

GAYLUSSACIA brachycera, R
(box huckleberry)
COLOR: white
HEIGHT: to 1 ft., stems creeping
BLOOM: spring
SOIL: sandy, peaty
SHADE: light to full
REMARKS: similar to Vaccinium,

which is deciduous. Blue fruits. Native.

ILEX crenata (Japanese holly)
HEIGHT: to 20 ft.
SOIL: good garden
SHADE: full but not dense
REMARKS: excellent hedge, ground cover and specimen resembling boxwood. Does well in city. Var. convexa grows broader than tall. Var. microphylla has very small leaves, but is erect growing. Var. helleri, spreading, remains usually under two feet, but can in 25 years reach 4 ft. Some miniature mounds are var. stokes, hetzi, 'Green Island,' 'Kingsville' and 'Kingsville Green Cushion.' Japan.

ILEX glabra (inkberry)
HEIGHT: to 8 ft.
BLOOM: June-July. Inconspicuous
SOIL: good, peaty, sandy, moist
SHADE: light
REMARKS: tolerant in cities. Thrifty. Black berries, fruiting plants should be obtained. Stands pruning well. There is a compact form. Native.

ILEX opaca (American holly)
COLOR: greenish yellow, inconspicuous

HEIGHT: to 50 ft.
BLOOM: June, inconspicuous
SOIL: well drained
SHADE: light
REMARKS: prune heavily or remove at least half the leaves when transplanting. Berries red. Fruiting plants should be obtained. Native. The English Holly is more beautiful but not reliable for hardiness north of New York City. Even American holly may need protection north of this area.

KALMIA latifolia
(mountain-laurel, calico-bush)

COLOR: rose to white
HEIGHT: to 10 ft. or more
BLOOM: May, June
SOIL: moist, peaty, or sandy, acid
SHADE: any, not deep for good bloom
REMARKS: fine evergreen whose leaves do not curl in winter. Keep mulched all year. Native.

LEIOPHYLLUM buxifolium, R
(sand-myrtle)

COLOR: white or pinkish
HEIGHT: under 2 ft.
BLOOM: May
SOIL: moist, peaty, sandy, loam

SHADE: half
REMARKS: borders, ground cover, small leaves. Plant in clumps. Native.

LEUCOTHOË catesbaei
(drooping leucothoë)

COLOR: white
HEIGHT: to 6 ft., usually lower
BLOOM: April, May
SOIL: moist, peaty, sandy
SHADE: any
REMARKS: foliage turns bronze-purple in winter sun. Flowers in drooping racemes. Other species will also grow in shade. Native. L. axillaris is compact and lower growing.

MAHONIA aquifolium
(holly-mahonia)

COLOR: yellow spikes
HEIGHT: to 3 ft. or more
BLOOM: May
SOIL: good garden
SHADE: light to half
REMARKS: lustrous foliage, protect from winter sun and too much wind. Blue berries. Native.

MAHONIA repens, R
(creeping-mahonia)

COLOR: yellow spikes

MAHONIA repens, R—*cont.*
HEIGHT: to 1 ft.
BLOOM: May
SOIL: good garden
SHADE: light
REMARKS: blue-black berries late summer and fall, ground cover. Native.

PACHISTIMA canbyi, R
(mountain-lover, pachistima)
COLOR: flowers inconspicuous
HEIGHT: to 1 ft.
BLOOM: April, May
SOIL: well drained, acid
SHADE: light
REMARKS: narrow, dainty leaves, reddish in winter, ground cover. Native.

PIERIS floribunda [Andromeda floribunda]
(mountain andromeda)
COLOR: white or cream
HEIGHT: to 6 ft.
BLOOM: April-May
SOIL: moist, porous, humus, preferably acid
SHADE: light
REMARKS: greenish-white flower buds all winter. Plant less attractive than P. japonica, and more difficult to keep in good health but hardier than the Japanese species. Native.

PIERIS japonica [Andromeda japonica]
(Japanese andromeda)
COLOR: white
HEIGHT: to 10 ft.
BLOOM: April, May
SOIL: moist, humus, porous, preferably acid
SHADE: light
REMARKS: reddish flower clusters seem ready to burst into bloom all winter. Handsomer than P. floribunda. Japan.

PYRACANTHA coccinea lalandi
(laland firethorn)
COLOR: white, small
HEIGHT: to 20 ft.
BLOOM: June
SOIL: good garden
SHADE: half
REMARKS: good hedge, not too closely planted. Will not berry in the shade. Leaves are small and glossy. When trained against walls it receives protection sometimes needed in the north. Orange-red fruits. S. Europe, W. Asia.

RHODODENDRON species, varieties and hybrids.
(rhododendron and azalea)
COLOR: white, lavender, fuchsia,

purple, orange, rose, pink, salmon, yellow
HEIGHT: 1 to 36 feet
BLOOM: May, June, July
SHADE: full, light, half
REMARKS: there are hundreds of rhododendrons (evergreen) and azaleas (mostly deciduous) to be had, many are fragrant. A few are discussed below. See also under Azalea (evergreen and deciduous).

RHODODENDRON carolinianum
(Carolina rhododendron)
COLOR: pale rose-purple to white
HEIGHT: to 6 ft.
BLOOM: May-June
SOIL: damp, loose, acid, humus
SHADE: half
REMARKS: compact habit, small leaves. Native.

RHODODENDRON catawbiense
(mountain rose bay, catawba rhododendron)
COLOR: lilac-purple
HEIGHT: to 20 ft.
BLOOM: June
SOIL: damp, loose, acid, humus
SHADE: light to full
REMARKS: one of the most beautiful native shrubs, but a difficult color. Var. alba has white flowers.

RHODODENDRON maximum
(great laurel, rosebay rhododendron)
COLOR: white, spotted with green on upper lip
HEIGHT: to 35 ft.
BLOOM: June-July
SOIL: damp, loose, acid, humus
SHADE: almost any
REMARKS: very hardy. Background planting. Native.

SARCOCOCCA hookeriana humilis
(fragrant S.)
COLOR: white, fragrant
HEIGHT: to 1 ½ ft., usually less
BLOOM: very early spring
SOIL: good garden
SHADE: almost any
REMARKS: fine as spreading ground cover. Narrow, glossy evergreen leaves on short stems. May be somewhat tender. China.

TAXUS baccata repandens
(spreading English yew)
HEIGHT: nearly prostrate
SOIL: any good
SHADE: light
REMARKS: ground cover, broad coverage. Red berries fall and winter. Europe, N. Africa, W. Asia.

TAXUS canadensis
(ground-hemlock, American yew,
Canada yew, ground yew)

HEIGHT: seldom over 3 ft.
SOIL: any good
SHADE: any
REMARKS: branches spread in all
directions. Rather straggling. Red
berries in August. Native.

TAXUS cuspidata
(Japanese yew)
and its forms

HEIGHT: to 40 ft.
SOIL: any good
SHADE: light
REMARKS: many var. vase-shaped,
low mounded and miniatures.
Far East.

TAXUS media
(yew)

HEIGHT: to 40 feet
SOIL: good garden
SHADE: light
REMARKS: cross between T.
baccata and T. cuspidata. Forms

are conical, erect and dense, or
erect and loose. Mostly red
fruiting.

THUJA occidentalis
(American arbor-vitæ)

HEIGHT: to 60 ft.
SOIL: good moist
SHADE: light
REMARKS: there are many forms
of this, some very dwarf. Small
brown cones. Will stand crowd-
ing against other shrubs or
against buildings. Soil must be
moist. Var. semperaurea with
golden-tip leaves is especially
shade resistant. Native.

TSUGA canadensis and other species
(hemlock)

HEIGHT: to 60 ft.
SOIL: good moist
SHADE: any
REMARKS: one of the few evergreens which will stand full
shade, and probably the most
beautiful. Native.

VINES, DECIDUOUS AND EVERGREEN

ACTINIDIA arguta
(bower A.)
COLOR: white, inconspicuous
HEIGHT: 20 ft. or more

SOIL: rich, somewhat moist
SHADE: half
REMARKS: rapid-growing, decid-
uous, twining by stems. Screens,

trellises, arbors. Young leaves which grow to 6 in. long are silvery. Far East.

AKEBIA quinata (five-leaf akebia)

COLOR: mauve
HEIGHT: 30 to 40 ft.
BLOOM: May
SOIL: good garden
SHADE: half to light
REMARKS: twining, dainty if kept in control, half evergreen. Vine or ground cover. Far East.

AMPELOPSIS brevipedunculata
(porcelain ampelopsis)

BLOOM: small, greenish
SOIL: loamy
SHADE: half
REMARKS: walls, rocks, trellises. Climbs by tendrils. Beautiful berries lilac becoming blue. N.E. Asia.

ARISTOLOCHIA durior [A. macro-phylla] (Dutchman's-pipe)

COLOR: yellowish-green, brownish-purple
HEIGHT: to 30 ft.
BLOOM: May
SOIL: good, loamy, sweet
SHADE: half
REMARKS: round leaves 10 in. in diameter. Good as screen. Twining by stems, woody. Native.

CELASTRUS scandens
(American bitter-sweet, waxwork)

COLOR: greenish, inconspicuous
HEIGHT: 20 ft. or more
SOIL: any good
SHADE: light to half
REMARKS: climbing by twining stems, woody. Fruits orange-yellow. For fruits, use fruiting plants (female). Native.

CLEMATIS, many species esp. large flowered hybrids

COLOR: white, shades of red, pink, mauve, purple, two toned, etc.
HEIGHT: erect to 6 ft., or climbing to 30 ft.
BLOOM: spring, summer, autumn
SOIL: fertile, light, loamy, well drained. Add spadeful of lime to each barrow of soil
SHADE: base in shade, but plant must climb into sun or half shade
REMARKS: many have huge flowers and decorative anthers. Mulch with leaves, straw, peat, moss or decayed manure in fall to check winter killing.

CLEMATIS paniculata
(sweet autumn C.)

COLOR: white
HEIGHT: 30 feet

BLOOM: late August, September
SOIL: moist, some lime
SHADE: half
REMARKS: clouds of tiny star-like blossoms. Very fragrant, climbs by twisting leaf stalks. Plumy silver seed heads. Japan.

CLEMATIS verticillaris
(purple virgins-bower)
COLOR: blue-purple, or rose-purple
HEIGHT: to 10 ft.
BLOOM: May-June
SOIL: rich, moist, some lime
SHADE: half, must be allowed to climb into the sun or half shade
REMARKS: this species sometimes blooms beautifully even in light shade. Climbs by twining leaf stalk. Native.

CLEMATIS virginiana
(virgins-bower, old mans-beard)
COLOR: white, greenish
HEIGHT: climbing to 20 ft.
BLOOM: August-September
SOIL: rich, loamy, moist, some lime
SHADE: half, must be allowed to climb into the sun
REMARKS: drapes itself charmingly over bushes. Climbs by twisting leaf stalks. Native.

EUONYMUS. See under "Evergreen Shrubs."

HEDERA helix (English ivy)
HEIGHT: 30-40 ft.
SOIL: rich
SHADE: any
REMARKS: woody vine climbing by adhesive disks or trailing. Good ground cover. Var. arborescens is erect and does not climb. There are several miniature leaf varieties, all may need protection north. Var. baltica is very hardy, as is a variety called '238th Street.' Europe, Asia, N. Africa.

HYDRANGEA petiolaris
(climbing hydrangea)
COLOR: white
HEIGHT: to 50 ft.
BLOOM: June, July
SOIL: rich, porous, somewhat moist
SHADE: half to light
REMARKS: woody vine, climbs by holdfasts onto walls. Handsome trained as a specimen shrub, or ground cover. Japan.

LATHYRUS latifolius and its forms
(perennial or everlasting pea)
COLOR: rose, dark purple and red, white

HEIGHT: climbing to 9 ft.
BLOOM: July-September
SOIL: common garden
SHADE: light
REMARKS: pea-shaped flowers in clusters. Good for banks, stumps, etc. Europe.

LONICERA henryi
(Henry honeysuckle)

COLOR: yellowish red to purplish
HEIGHT: twining or prostrate
BLOOM: June, July
SOIL: good garden
SHADE: light to half
REMARKS: half evergreen. Similar to but less rampageous than Hall's H., though hardier. Black persistent berries. Will climb on anything in sight. China.

LONICERA japonica halliana
(Hall's honeysuckle)

COLOR: white changing to yellowish, purplish outside
HEIGHT: to 15 ft.
BLOOM: July, August
SOIL: good garden
SHADE: light
REMARKS: grows anywhere, climber and good ground cover. Too rampageous for most gardens, twining on anything nearby. China, Japan, naturalized in America.

LONICERA sempervirens
(trumpet honeysuckle)

COLOR: scarlet, yellow inside
HEIGHT: 20 ft. or more
BLOOM: May-August
SOIL: normal
SHADE: half
REMARKS: attractive flowers, ground cover. Red fruits. Climbs by twining. Native.

PARTHENOCISSUS quinquefolia
[Ampelopsis quinquefolia and hederacea] (Virginia creeper, woodbine, American ivy)

COLOR: yellowish or greenish, inconspicuous
HEIGHT: 12 ft. or more
BLOOM: summer
SOIL: rich
SHADE: any but dense
REMARKS: clinging to trees, walls, buildings, or a ground cover. Var. saint-pauli clings better, smaller leaves. Fruits bluish-black in September and October. Fine autumn color. Native.

PARTHENOCISSUS tricuspidata
[Ampelopsis]
(Boston ivy, Japanese ivy)

HEIGHT: high climbing

SOIL: good garden
SHADE: any
REMARKS: clings to wood or masonry unaided. Japan, China.

POLYGONUM aubertii
(silver lace vine, fleece vine)

COLOR: white
HEIGHT: 20 feet or more
BLOOM: late summer
SOIL: good garden
SHADE: half to light
REMARKS: rapid grower by twining, must be pruned to keep in bounds. Fragrant. P. baldschuanicum has larger rose-colored flowers. China.

PUERARIA thunbergiana
(kudzu-vine)

COLOR: purple
HEIGHT: to 60 ft.
BLOOM: late summer
SHADE: half
REMARKS: pea-shaped flowers. Rapid and coarse grower by twining, on verandas, arbors, thick screen. Fragrant. Probably will die to ground in winter though hardy. Japan, China.

VITIS labrusca and others
(fox grape)

SOIL: humus or any good garden
SHADE: light to full
REMARKS: climbing by tendrils. Black berries with bluish bloom September and October. Fragrant. Wild garden. Will endure city conditions. Native.

WISTERIA floribunda
(Japanese wisteria)

COLOR: violet-blue, violet, white, pink, reddish
BLOOM: May
SOIL: deep rich
SHADE: light
REMARKS: can be grown as a tree-like shrub, will not bloom in the shade but will climb up into the treetops and bloom when it reaches a sunny area. Worth growing for its vigorous habit and attractive leaves. Twines by stems. Japan. There is a native species, W. frutescens, which will bloom in half to light shade. Chinese W. has shorter flower racemes. The white var. very fragrant. Far East.

HERBS. See page 70.
HOUSE PLANTS. See page 135.